GW00760319

My Pregnancy

This book has been published by the HSE (2018). This is the second edition (2020). It is given to all parents-to-be.

My Pregnancy is filled with expert advice from health professionals in the HSE, including doctors, midwives, nurses, physiotherapists, dietitians, psychologists and many more.

Our team, led by Dr Fiona McGuire, has worked to give you the best advice on caring for yourself and your baby during your pregnancy, labour and birth.

After the birth, you will receive 2 other books from your public health nurse:

- My Child: 0 to 2 years
- My Child: 2 to 5 years

All of the information in these books, and more, is online at mychild.ie

We hope that you can use these books and the website as a companion for every step from pregnancy through your child's first 5 years.

What parents-to-be said

We asked parents-to-be what information would help them most during pregnancy. They told us the most important topics they wanted included.

They also asked for:

- common sense information and tips on pregnancy
- advice on what to do if they had a problem
- details of which people and services to get in touch with for more help and support

They also told us they wanted this information to be available online and in a printed version to keep at home.

Experience and knowledge

The advice in this book and on mychild.ie is based on the most up-to-date information available within the health service, and on the experience and knowledge of maternal and child health and support services, voluntary organisations and parent groups.

Help every step of the way

Whether you are expecting a baby for the first time, or you have done this before, we want to help you every step of the way.

We are so grateful to everyone who helped to create these books, especially the parents.

For more information on pregnancy and child health, visit mychild.ie

First published: 2018 (version 1.0)
Updated: 2020 (version 2.0)
This 2020 edition (version 2.0) has updated information on vitamin D supplements for babies (page 159).
Updates are made to individual sections when we become aware of changes to health guidelines or advice.
Reviews take place every few years when the entire book is reviewed by experts.

ISBN: 978-1-78602-114-4

Contents

Starting your journey

To pregnant mothers

Congratulations! You are about to become a parent, maybe for the first time. It is a time of great change — to your body, your emotions and your life. It is also a special time in your life where you will be adapting to your role as a parent. Nothing will ever be quite the same again.

During the months of your pregnancy there may be a number of challenges. It is important to build supports around you. These are your partner or support person, family, friends and healthcare professionals.

This support will help you:

- to adapt
- to feel emotionally and physically prepared for the birth of your baby

We hope that this book will:

- answer some of the questions that you may have
- help you take care of yourself as you look forward to the arrival of your new baby

To fathers-to-be, mothers-to-be, partners, spouses and support persons

Congratulations! You are about to become a parent, maybe for the first time. We know that 21st century families come in all shapes and sizes. Your relationship and support will help your pregnant partner.

This is a time of great change as you adjust to your new role.

We hope that you will:

- read this book together
- use it to talk about pregnancy, birth and parenthood
- learn how you can be supportive to each other

There is so much you can do to help. This is a journey upon which you will embark together.

To grandparents, families and friends

Congratulations! A new little person is about to join your family.

Your support will be needed and greatly appreciated during the pregnancy and your loved one's journey to parenthood.

A map of your journey

Week 0 to 12

"I'm going to have a baby!"

- See GP or community midwife as early as possible to confirm pregnancy and discuss care options.
- Take folic acid.
- Consider getting the flu vaccine.
- Attend maternity unit or hospital for first antenatal appointment and dating scan.

By the end of the first trimester your baby is as big as a lime!

Week 13 to 28

"What will my baby be like?"

At this stage, you should:

- Continue GP and hospital appointments.
- From 16 weeks protect your baby from whooping cough by getting the vaccine.
- Fill in maternity benefit form after 24 weeks.

You might also:

- Get a fetal anatomy scan at 18 to 22 weeks.
- Be screened for diabetes from 24 to 28 weeks.
- Begin thinking of your baby's name.

By the end of the second trimester your baby is as big as a head of lettuce!

Week 29 to 40

"I'm preparing to become a parent."

- GP and hospital appointments become more frequent.
- Antenatal classes begin.
- Begin preparation for birth and your baby's arrival.
- Tune in to your baby's movements.
- Think about your birth options and preferences, but keep an open mind.

By week 40 your baby is as big as a watermelon!

After the birth

"I'm a parent!"

- Enjoy safe skin-to-skin contact.
- Most babies are ready to breastfeed soon after birth.
- Your baby will be offered vitamin K.
- Your midwife will examine your baby at birth.
- A doctor or specially trained midwife will do a full clinical examination of your baby within 72 hours of birth.
- Your baby will have other screening tests done — such as the heel prick and hearing screening.
- You will be preparing to bring your baby home.

Your pregnancy and you

You're about to become a parent, maybe for the first time. This is a time of great change both inside and outside your body.

You may already be starting to connect with your baby. This will help you form a strong bond with your baby after they are born.

Bonding with your bump

Your voice

Use everyday activities to talk to your bump. Encourage your partner to talk too. You may notice that your baby gets quiet or starts to move when they hear certain voices.

Songs and music

Singing songs and lullabies to your baby may help soothe them. Playing calm and soothing music can also have the same effect.

Gently rock and move in time to music. This will help your baby develop good motor skills and balance.

You may notice that the same music will help your baby to calm down and relax after birth.

Touch

Touching and stroking your bump gently is another good way to bond with your baby. Notice how your baby responds to your touch.

Imagine you are meeting your baby for the first time. Visualise your baby. What image comes to mind when you think of your child?

Did you know?

Your baby can sense how you are feeling by your heartbeat and by the hormones you release. For example, when you are calm and relaxed, your baby will be calm also.

The birth of a parent

As well as being a time for babies to grow and develop, pregnancy is also a time when parents are born.

Even if this is not your first baby, your family is growing and changing. Your parenting style will need to adjust to accommodate the needs of a new baby in addition to older children.

Your time

As parents, pregnancy is your time. It is your time to think, to grow and to prepare. The physical changes of pregnancy become obvious as time passes. The emotional journey taken by a parent is more private and occurs in the mind.

Emotional changes

You will experience emotional changes during pregnancy. Tiredness, nausea and hormones during pregnancy can affect how you feel. It is normal to have a range of feelings and emotions.

These could be positive and negative. They may include:

- joy
- excitement
- uncertainty
- feelings of upheaval — like your world has been turned upside-down
- anxiety or worrying
- ambivalence — not entirely sure you want to become a parent

Support your mental wellbeing

Try to do things that will support your mental wellbeing during pregnancy. This includes eating healthy foods, taking exercise, getting enough sleep and doing something you enjoy, like reading, music or yoga.

You may need extra support.
Talk to your GP, midwife or obstetrician if:

- your initial feelings of uncertainty and ambivalence do not settle
- you have high levels of anxiety
- your mood is low

Thoughts and feelings you may have:

- What will it be like to be a parent?
- What kind of parent will I be?
- What type of parent will my partner be?
- What type of grandparent will my mother or father become?
- If you have a partner, you may feel more like a family now that one of you is pregnant.
- At work, or socially, you may find yourselves identifying more with colleagues and friends who are pregnant or have children.

Dealing with change

You and your partner or support person may have lots of thoughts and feelings about change.

The more support you have, the easier you may find it to process the positive and the negative thoughts and feelings that you have.

Think about your support network (family, friends and neighbours). When you become a parent you need practical support. You also need understanding and sensitivity to help you adjust to this change.

Your feelings and emotions

Pregnancy is a time of change for your body, your mind and your life. It is normal to have a range of emotions during your pregnancy.

- Your body is changing.
- Your emotions are changing.
- People may be treating you differently.
- You may think differently.
- You may be thinking more about your new baby and your future.
- You may feel anxious.
- You may be having mood swings.

All of this is normal.

What you can do

Take care of yourself

- Eat well.
- Take a multivitamin with folic acid suitable for pregnancy.
- Be as active as you can.
- Get enough sleep.

Talk to people

- Talk to the people you feel closest to about your feelings.
- It's ok to ask questions. If you are worried about anything, ask your GP, midwife or obstetrician.

Be kind to yourself

- Rest when you need to, reduce your household chores and get help when you can.
- Do something you enjoy, like reading, listening to music, yoga.
- Take time to laugh and enjoy life.

Your support network

Build your support network. Some people have more support than others. Your support network could be your partner, your family or your friends.

Not sure you want to be pregnant?

If you are pregnant but not sure you want to be, you can talk to your GP or a HSE-funded crisis pregnancy counselling service. Visit sexualwellbeing.ie for information.

If you are suffering from depression or have ever suffered from depression or post-natal depression, you need to tell your doctor and midwife. They can offer support and monitor you closely during this pregnancy.

When to get help

It is very important to talk to your GP, midwife or obstetrician if you have any of these symptoms for more than 2 weeks:

- worrying more than usual and feeling anxious
- severe anxiety
- losing interest in your usual activities
- feeling down, sad or hopeless
- physical symptoms like panic attacks or palpitations

Mental health problems

Mental health problems in pregnancy are common. Some women may find previous mental health issues resurface during pregnancy. Others may experience mental health difficulties for the first time while pregnant.

If either of these applies to you, talk to your midwife or GP at any time during pregnancy. There is help, support and treatment available.

Some women worry about telling healthcare professionals about mental health difficulties. They can be afraid that they will be judged or that their baby might be taken away from them.

Do not let this fear get in the way of finding help. Healthcare professionals like your GP or midwife will be sympathetic and supportive. They will work hard to help you to get well. This will help you to care for your baby.

Remember:

- It is not your fault.
- You are not alone.
- There is help available.

Your support network

"It takes a village to raise a child" is a traditional African proverb. It refers to our need for help from other members of the community to support our children as they grow.

Nowadays life is highly pressured, fast-paced and more stressful than ever. Navigating parenthood can be a difficult and overwhelming task. Never has our village been more needed, yet more difficult to find.

Think about your 'village'. Who is your support network? If possible, identify one or two people you can call on for help at any hour, even if it's just for a chat. It is okay to ask for help. People want to help out at this special time. Be specific about what you need.

Talk to the people you feel closest to about your feelings and concerns. This will help you to put things in perspective and help you to cope.

Ways your friends and family can help after the baby is born

- Bring food – nutritious meals that you can just heat up.
- Bring healthy snacks like fruit and water.
- Do laundry.
- Take your other children out for a few hours.
- Encourage you to leave the house – for example, meeting you for a cup of tea or a walk.
- Hold the baby while you take a nap.
- Give you space to talk and allow you to share your joy but also to complain if that is what you need. We all need the chance to celebrate but we also need a good moan at times!

Finding support as a lone parent

There are over 200,000 one-parent families in Ireland today. Every year thousands of people experience pregnancy alone. This can happen for many reasons:

- Maybe your relationship with your partner has ended, through death or divorce or because they no longer wish to be involved.
- Maybe you are single and have chosen to have a baby alone using donor sperm or another method.
- Maybe you are geographically separated from your partner.

Whatever your unique story, you are setting off on this journey without a partner. This may seem like an overwhelming task at times.

Build a support system

Remember, you may not have to travel this journey alone. Build a support system. Do you have close family, or friends you could lean on? Your family and friends will often be more than willing to support you.

Sharing your news

Sometimes sharing the news of your pregnancy can be difficult when you are a lone parent. For example, if you are in your teens and it happened earlier than planned, or if there are difficult circumstances.

Finding out you are pregnant is a life-changing experience. Tell a friend or two before the news becomes obvious. This means you are in control of who you share your news with.

Local support groups

Unfortunately, not all of us can be near loving family and friends. If this is the case, speak to your midwife. See if your local hospital offers support groups for lone parents.

As well as being educational, antenatal classes are a great way of meeting other expectant parents.

For fathers and partners

Pregnancy can be a wonderful and exhilarating time, but sometimes it can be difficult.

Partners, your role is important. You can provide support, advocate for your partner, provide a shoulder to cry on and, of course, get the (healthy) snacks!

How partners can help

Ask and provide support

- Ask her how you can help.
- Get informed by doing some research about pregnancy and birth – this book is a great place to start!
- Talk to your partner about breastfeeding and encourage it. Breastfeeding is the healthiest way to feed your baby.
- Be there! Go with her to antenatal appointments and antenatal classes if possible. What you learn can help during the birth.
- Tell her she's beautiful. Pregnancy can cause many changes to a woman's body, and she may feel insecure about these changes.
- Listen to her. Be patient — she may be emotional at times.
- Understand that she may be less interested in sex, or her libido may increase at times.

Talk about the birth and the baby

- Talk about how she wants to give birth. You can help support these wishes when she is in labour.
- Discuss your baby and how you want to parent.
- Think about your new role as a parent. This is an important role that is vital to your baby.

Help out

- Share household chores and maybe do a few extra ones without being asked. Growing a baby is hard work and she may not have enough hours in her day.
- If you have a cat, change the cat litter tray.
- Bring out the bins.
- Carry things that are too heavy for her, for example food shopping.
- If you have other children, bring them out on trips to give her a break.

Be healthy together

New her, new you!

- The best way to help her quit smoking is to stop yourself. This will be healthier for you and your new baby. Don't smoke around her.
- Join your partner by eating healthily together.
- Help her not to drink alcohol by planning activities that don't revolve around drinking. Go on walks or to the cinema instead. Try not to drink around her too often.
- Encourage her to be active. Maybe exercise together?

Bonding with your unborn baby

Feel for kicks – a few weeks after your partner experiences the baby moving, you will be able to feel it too.

Listen to your baby's heartbeat at antenatal appointments.

Talk or sing to your baby – even in the womb, your baby will recognise your voice and react to it.

Don't worry if it takes you longer than your partner to feel that special connection. This is normal.

Did you know?

Research looked at fathers and parents who interacted more with their children in their first few months after birth. It found they could have a positive impact on their baby's brain development.

Helping hands along the way

Healthcare professionals you may meet along the way

GP

A GP (general practitioner) is a family doctor who cares for you during and after your pregnancy. They care for families, babies, and children.

Midwife

They care for you during pregnancy and support you during labour and birth. Your midwife cares for you and your baby in the first few days after birth. They help you with breastfeeding.

Obstetrician

An obstetrician is a doctor who cares for you during pregnancy, labour and birth. Not every pregnancy or birth needs an obstetrician.

Lactation consultant

They support and help the breastfeeding mother and her baby. Not all maternity hospitals have lactation consultants.

Anaesthetist

They are doctors who care for you if you need an epidural or a caesarean birth.

Public health nurse (PHN)

When you come home from the hospital, the PHN will visit you within 72 hours. They will examine you and your baby. The PHN is there to support you and your family.

GP practice nurse

They work with your GP to care for you during and after your pregnancy. They care for families, babies, and children. In many practices the nurse will give your baby their vaccines.

Special care baby unit or neonatal unit nurse

They care for babies who need specialised care after birth.

Dietician

The dietician promotes healthy eating habits. They may need to develop a specific diet for you if you have a medical condition such as diabetes.

Physiotherapist

A physiotherapist with an interest in women's health will help you after the birth if you have trouble moving around normally or if you are having certain problems with your pelvis, bowels or bladder. Physiotherapy can help you to recover after the birth.

Neonatologist

They are doctors who care for newborn babies. In some hospitals, this is done by paediatricians.

Paediatricians

A paediatrician is a doctor who cares for babies and for older children.

Medical social worker

They provide assistance to families with financial or social needs.

Pharmacist

Pharmacists are sometimes called chemists. They are experts in medicines and how you should use them. They have in-depth knowledge on how medicines affect your body. You can visit your pharmacist to ask them for advice about common pregnancy complaints or about medicines you may need to take.

Antenatal care

Your options

The care you receive during pregnancy from healthcare professionals is called antenatal care. This helps you have a healthy pregnancy and baby.

Types of antenatal care

Every pregnant woman living in Ireland or intending to live here for at least one year is entitled to free antenatal care under the Maternity and Infant Care scheme.

Some people prefer to pay for private or semi-private care. Your GP visits will still be covered by the Maternity and Infant Care scheme.

Shared or combined antenatal care

Many people opt for 'combined' or shared antenatal care.

This means you attend your GP and see your midwife or obstetrician in the maternity hospital or home birth midwife if you are having a home birth.

You will need to register with your GP for the Maternity and Infant Care Scheme.

Where to give birth

You might have a choice between a hospital or home birth. This will depend on where you live.

Getting support on your journey

These are the options you may have:

Different types of shared or combined care:

Supported care	You can choose to birth your baby in a hospital or at home.	Your care will be provided by midwives.	This type of care is suitable for most people with uncomplicated pregnancies.
Assisted care	The birth will take place in a hospital.	Your care will be provided by obstetricians and midwives.	This type of care is suitable if your pregnancy is less straightforward or if you want a doctor-led service (for example, if you want an epidural).
Other assisted care options	If you choose to have an obstetrician leading your care, you may have the option of public, semi-private or private care. Your GP will discuss this with you.		
Specialised care	The birth will take place in a hospital.	Your care will be provided by obstetricians and midwives.	This type of care will be recommended to people with higher risk pregnancies.

Other free public options you may have (depending on your location):

Domino scheme

This is a midwife-led scheme available in some hospitals. Your care will be provided by a team of midwives. You will usually be transferred home within 12 to 24 hours of birth. After that a midwife will visit you in your home.

Home births

A home birth means giving birth at home with the support of a midwife. A planned home birth can be a safe alternative to a planned hospital birth for some pregnancies.

Making the decision

The decision can be made by you, your midwife, your GP and other medical advisors. You will need to talk about whether this option is safe for you and your baby. You will also need to book at a maternity hospital of your choice.

Registering

The HSE provides a home birth service through self-employed community midwives. You should register with a GP for the Maternity and Infant Care Scheme and book at a maternity hospital of your choice.

Your care

An important part of the care you receive is getting information. This will help you make informed choices about your pregnancy and birth.

Antenatal checks

Regular antenatal checks you can expect if you choose shared or combined antenatal care:

- Your urine and blood pressure will be checked at every antenatal appointment. Your weight may be checked.
- At later appointments after 20 weeks, the doctor or midwife will also examine your tummy to check the position of your baby. They may also measure the height of your womb (uterus). They will ask you about your baby's movements at every visit after 20 weeks. They may listen to your baby's heartbeat.

GP

You will see your GP at least five times during pregnancy, usually at the GP surgery. They will do regular antenatal checks.

First visit with your GP

See your GP as early as possible to confirm your pregnancy. They will discuss your options and refer you for antenatal care.

They will also give you information on how to have a healthy pregnancy.

They might discuss folic acid, exercise, healthy eating and vaccinations.

They can help if you need support to stop smoking or drinking alcohol.

Flu vaccine

The flu vaccine can be given at any stage.

16 to 36 weeks

They will give you a vaccination to protect your baby from whooping cough (pertussis).

Obstetrician

You will see your obstetrician for antenatal care in the hospital if your GP or midwife has a particular concern or if this is your preference. They will do regular antenatal checks.

At the booking visit

They may perform your dating scan or refer you for this.

20 to 22 weeks

You may be offered an anatomy (anomaly) scan.

If you need extra monitoring

You may get extra monitoring if you:

- have certain medical conditions
- have had complications in a previous pregnancy
- your GP or midwife is concerned

Midwife

You will see your midwife at least five times during pregnancy for antenatal care. This will be in the hospital or at home, depending on where you choose. They will do regular antenatal checks if this is your preference.

At the booking visit

Your midwife will ask detailed questions about your medical and family history and any previous pregnancies. They will also arrange blood tests and talk to you about antenatal classes and breastfeeding.

They will record your weight and height.

28 weeks

They will talk to you about breastfeeding. They will also talk to you about anti-D if you are 'rhesus negative' (see page 25).

36 weeks

They will talk to you about your birth wishes.

38 weeks

Your midwife will talk to you about preparing for the birth.

Tell your doctor or midwife if you:

- had complications in a previous pregnancy or any of your births
- have medical conditions
- have a family history of an inherited disease like cystic fibrosis or if the baby's father has

How to get the most of your antenatal care

Attend all your appointments

This care is very important for you and your baby.

Encourage your partner to attend

This may help them feel more involved in the pregnancy.

Ask questions

When you go to see your doctor or your midwife it is quite normal to feel a little overwhelmed. Sometimes all of the questions that you had been planning to ask disappear from your head!

If you have any questions or concerns, write them down on a list and bring this to the appointment.

Be prepared

Waiting times may vary. This can be difficult, especially if you have children with you. Bring a snack and something to read, and something to entertain the small people!

Bear in mind that some hospitals do not allow children at antenatal clinics, so check this prior to your appointment.

Additional needs

Let your doctor or midwife know if you have additional needs. For example, language difficulties, reduced hearing or eyesight or difficulty moving.

A note on students

Some of the healthcare professionals you see will be accompanied by students. They may be at different stages of their education.

As well as helping them to become a better doctor, midwife or nurse, you may find that having students around enhances your experience.

You can say "no" if you would prefer not to have a student present.

Your service, your say

When it comes to your health or your baby's health, you have the right to say what you need to say, knowing that you are being listened to.

You have the right to give feedback about your experiences. You may occasionally wish to formally make a comment, give a compliment or make a complaint.

There are different options available on hse.ie.

Your Service Your Say

Antenatal classes

Antenatal classes prepare you for birth, breastfeeding and the transition to parenthood.

You will:

- get information and learn skills — helping you to make informed decisions about your labour, birth and parenting
- meet other parents-to-be
- have the opportunity to ask questions and express any concerns you may have

Classes are usually relaxed. They can be a good way to make friends with people expecting babies at similar times.

Choosing antenatal classes

Many maternity hospitals and health centres offer antenatal classes free of charge. Talk to your GP, midwife or your public health nurse about antenatal classes in your area.

Start thinking about this early in pregnancy and book your place. Classes may be full at the time you wish to attend.

In some areas there are private antenatal classes available. It is important to research the credentials of the course providers. Your midwife or GP may be able to advise if you find it hard to decide which classes to attend.

Speak to your midwife, public health nurse or GP if you cannot attend classes. They may have books, leaflets and DVDs that might help.

When classes start

Most antenatal classes start when you are between 26 to 32 weeks pregnant. If you are expecting twins or a multiple birth, consider starting classes early. Your babies may arrive early.

Pregnant women are entitled to take paid time off work to attend one set of antenatal classes. This is allowed under Section 8 of the Maternity Protection (Amendment) Act 2004.

Who is there

Classes usually involve midwives, public health nurses and physiotherapists, depending on the location.

Partners are usually welcome at classes. Check with your midwife before you go.

Some areas may run special antenatal classes for lone parents, teenagers and young adults.

Topics

The sessions are participant-led. This means that the members of the class decide the pace and have a say in the topics discussed in the class.

Topics may include physical and mental health during pregnancy, preparation for labour and birth, breastfeeding and becoming a parent.

Tests during pregnancy

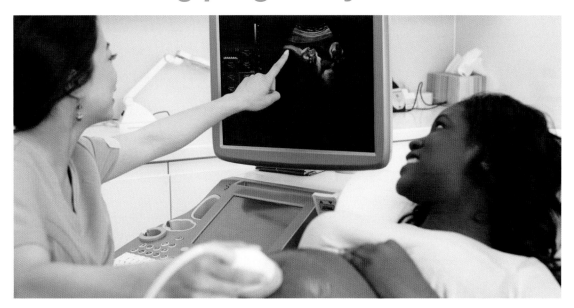

Blood tests

You will be offered blood tests as part of your antenatal care. These are important to make sure your pregnancy progresses safely and that your baby is healthy.

Talk to your doctor or midwife about these tests so you can make an informed choice about whether you want them or not.

This may seem like a lot of tests, but normally only one needle-stick is needed.

Full blood count

This is to check for anaemia. Anaemia is a condition. It is usually caused by low iron and can cause you to become very tired. It may cause other symptoms like breathlessness.

Blood group and antibodies

This is to check your blood and test for proteins called antibodies. The most important one of these is Rhesus (Rh) Factor.

If you are negative for Rhesus factor (Rhesus negative), and the baby's father is Rhesus positive, there is a chance that the baby could be Rhesus positive.

This could lead to your body producing antibodies against Rhesus. This will usually not affect this pregnancy, but might affect future ones.

Anti-D injections are safe and prevent Rhesus negative women from producing these antibodies.

Immunity to rubella (German measles)

If you get rubella in early pregnancy, it can be dangerous for your baby. If you have low immunity, you will be offered a vaccination after your baby is born.

Immunity to chickenpox

Many maternity units test your immunity to chickenpox, as this can be dangerous for pregnant women and babies. If you are not immune and come into contact with chickenpox, you need to contact your GP, obstetrican or midwife immediately.

Syphilis

You will be tested for this during pregnancy and offered treatment if you test positive.

Hepatitis B

If you have hepatitis B, there is a chance your baby could become infected. Vaccinating the baby at birth reduces this risk.

Hepatitis C

This virus can be passed to your baby. Unfortunately there is no way to prevent this. However, there are very effective treatments available for this virus. Your baby can be tested soon after birth.

HIV

If you are HIV positive, the birth will be managed to reduce the risk of infection to your baby. Your baby will be tested for HIV at birth and at intervals for up to two years. You will be advised not to breastfeed because HIV can be transmitted through breast milk.

What if I am afraid of needles?

Tell the person who is taking your blood for testing. They would prefer to know so that they can help to make it easier for you.

There are things you can do to help, like breathing exercises or distracting your thoughts.

You can get someone you trust to go along with you when you have these tests done.

Ultrasound scans

Ultrasound scans use sound waves to create a picture of your baby on a TV screen. The scans are safe and can be carried out at any stage of the pregnancy. They are not painful.

Gel is placed on your tummy and a small probe gently rubbed over it. This produces the picture on the screen.

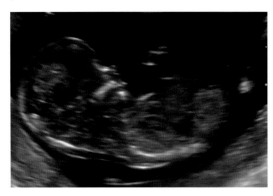

Dating scan

You will be offered a dating scan. Ideally this should be performed before 15 weeks.

Dating scans will detect:

- your baby's heartbeat
- the expected due date
- if you are expecting more than one baby

Fetal anatomy scan (anomaly scan)

Some pregnant women will be offered a fetal anatomy scan at 18 to 22 weeks. This is also called an anomaly scan.

Some hospitals offer this to every patient. Other hospitals only have the facilities to offer this to those with higher risk pregnancies.

Foetal anatomy scans can detect:

- If your baby is developing normally. Some babies can be hard to scan, because of the way they are lying in the womb.
- Birth defects like spina bifida and heart problems.

Unexpected news

Having a scan can be one of the highlights of your antenatal care. Finally you get to actually see your baby. You may even see their heart beating and limbs moving. You may even discover you are expecting two or even three babies.

For most people having an ultrasound scan is a happy and exciting event, but occasionally they can detect that your baby is unwell.

It is a good idea to bring your partner, family member or friend with you, in case you get unexpected news.

Additional scans

Scans are only performed when there is a medical reason for doing them. This means most pregnant women will probably only have one or two scans.

Most maternity hospitals do not perform scans to determine the sex of your baby.

You may have additional scans if:

- you have any bleeding
- there are any concerns about your baby's movements or growth

---

You may be given a printed photo of your baby at a scan. Don't leave it in sunlight or laminate it. The heat could damage the image.

Things to know before your scan

A full bladder

You will need a full bladder. In early pregnancy your womb can be quite small and lies quite low in the pelvis — that's the lower part of your body between your tummy and your thighs. A full bladder helps to push the womb upwards, making it easier for the scan to show what's inside it.

Drink water beforehand and bring some with you.

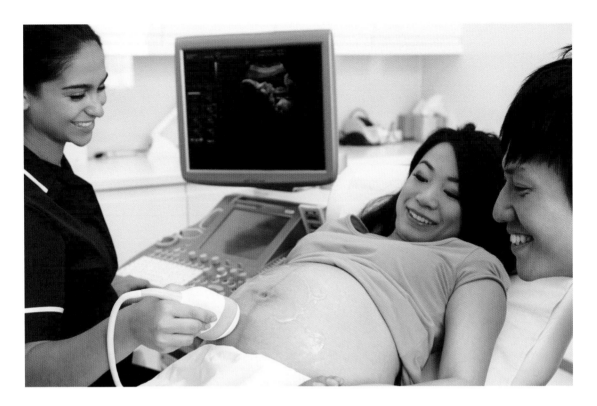

Who can come

Your partner or one support person can go along with you. Children are normally not allowed.

Filming

Recording devices like your mobile phone and cameras are normally not allowed.

Other specialised tests may be offered to you or you might decide to pay for extra ones.

Healthy pregnancy
Healthy eating

Healthy eating is important for pregnancy and breastfeeding. It provides your body with the nutrients it needs, which will help your baby to develop and grow.

You also need to make sure you get enough of certain nutrients such as:

- folic acid
- calcium
- vitamin D
- iron
- omega 3

These are especially important when you're pregnant — both for you and your baby.

As well as helping your baby, eating regular meals with a variety of foods will keep you healthy and strong.

'Eating for two' is just not true!
Being pregnant doesn't mean you should double the amount you eat.

Instead, eat:

- twice as healthily, not twice as much
- a normal amount and a balanced range of nutrients

The food pyramid

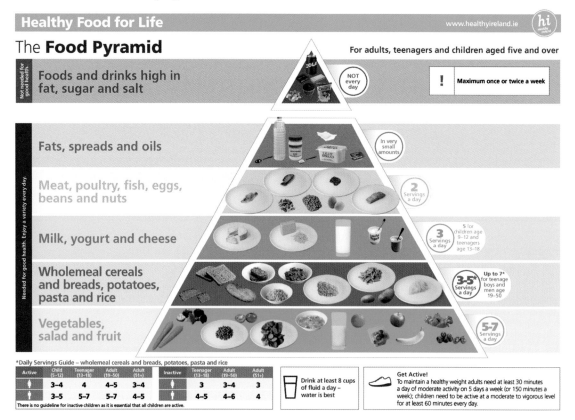

Source: Department of Health, December 2016.

Foods and drinks high in fat, sugar and salt

Small or fun-sized servings of chocolate, biscuits, cakes, sweets, crisps and other savoury snacks or ice cream. Not every day, maximum once or twice a week.

Fats, spreads and oils

1 serving is:

- 1 portion pack reduced-fat or light spread for 2 slices of bread
- 1 teaspoon oil per person when cooking

Meat, poultry, fish, eggs, beans and nuts

1 serving is:

- 50g to 75g cooked lean beef, lamb, pork, mince or poultry (half size of palm of hand)
- 100g cooked fish, soya or tofu
- 2 eggs, or
- ¾ cup beans or lentils

Milk, yogurt and cheese

1 serving is:

- 1 glass (200ml) milk
- 1 carton (125g) yogurt
- 2 thumbs (25g) hard cheese

Wholemeal cereals and breads, potatoes, pasta and rice

1 serving is:

- 2 thin slices wholemeal bread
- 1 cup cooked rice, pasta, noodles or cous cous
- 2 medium or 4 small potatoes

Vegetables, salad and fruit

1 serving is:

- 1 medium-sized fruit like an apple or banana
- ½ cup cooked vegetables

Nutrients for you and your baby

Iron

"This helps oxygen get around my little body, it also helps keep you healthy"

You should eat foods rich in iron at least twice per day during pregnancy.

Types of iron

Haem iron is more easily absorbed by the body. It is found in red meats like beef, lamb, mutton and pork.

Non-haem iron is harder for the body to absorb. It is found in eggs, green leafy vegetables, pulses and fortified breakfast cereals. Try and eat a variety of haem and non-haem sources of iron.

Vitamin C

Vitamin C helps your body to absorb iron. Try to eat foods rich in vitamin C with non-haem iron sources. Vitamin C foods include oranges, kiwis and strawberries.

Iron supplements

If blood tests show you have low iron levels, you might be prescribed a supplement.

Did you know?

Tea and coffee contain tannins. These can reduce the amount of iron your body absorbs. Avoid drinking tea and coffee with meals.

Folic acid

"It helps my spine develop normally"

Most pregnant women should take a folic acid supplement every day. It should contain 400 mcg of folic acid. Some people with certain medical conditions may need to take more. As well as taking a supplement, you should eat foods high in folic acid. These are:

- green leafy vegetables
- fortified breakfast cereals and milk

Omega 3

"This is important for my brain, nervous system and eyes. It protects you from heart disease"

You should eat 1 to 2 portions of oily fish each week. Oily fish includes salmon or mackerel.

Vegetarians should eat linseeds, rapeseed oil and walnuts. You may need a supplement if you are vegetarian or vegan or do not like oily fish.

Vitamin D

"I need this to keep my bones healthy. It may protect both of us from heart disease"

Vitamin D is called the sunshine vitamin. This is because your body can make it when strong sunlight falls on your skin. Unsurprisingly, people living in Ireland often have low vitamin D levels!

Oily fish like salmon and mackerel are naturally high in vitamin D. Eggs contain small amounts. Certain types of milk and many other foods have vitamin D – this is called 'fortified'.

Supplements

If you are worried about not getting enough vitamin D from your diet, consider taking a supplement. This should contain 10 micrograms of vitamin D.

If you are already taking a pregnancy multi-vitamin supplement, check the vitamin D content. Most pregnancy supplements contain enough vitamin D.

Don't take more than 10 micrograms of vitamin D unless you have been advised to do so by your GP, obstetrician or midwife.

Make sure you are not taking too much vitamin D.

Calcium

"This helps develop my skeleton. It also keeps your bones healthy"

Try to eat three servings per day of milk, cheese or yoghurt. These are rich in calcium and protein. Low fat dairy products contain similar amounts of calcium as full-fat versions.

One serving is a 200ml glass of milk, 2 thumbs (25g) of cheese or a 125g carton of yoghurt.

You should consider fortified non-dairy alternatives or a calcium and vitamin D supplement if you have:

- a dairy intolerance
- special dietary requirements like a vegan lifestyle

If you need a multi-vitamin or other supplement, make sure you take one specially designed for pregnancy.

Food aversions

A food aversion is a sense of disgust at a food you used to like. If there are healthy foods you can't stomach now, look for substitutes.

Cooking smells may be overpowering. If you can, ask someone else to cook. Cook with the windows open.

Food cravings

You may get cravings for particular foods during pregnancy. Try to include these as part of your meals, but avoid eating too much of any one food.

If you have a craving for a non-food item such as soap, dirt or chalk, talk to your GP, obstetrician or midwife.

Special diets

Vegetarian and vegan diets

If you are eating healthy and varied foods, your baby should get plenty of nutrients. However, many vegetarians and vegans can find it hard to get enough vitamin B12 and iron from food. If you are vegan, you also need to make sure you get enough vitamin D and calcium from your diet.

Vegan sources of iron:
- pulses like beans, lentils and peas
- dark green vegetables like spinach, broccoli and water cress
- apricots and other dried fruit
- fortified breakfast cereals (iron has been added to them)

Vegan sources of vitamin B12:
- fortified breakfast cereals
- yeast extract
- fortified and unsweetened milk alternatives like soya and oat milks

A vitamin B12 supplement may be needed.

Vegan sources of vitamin D:

In addition to sunlight, you can get vitamin D from:

- fortified breakfast cereals
- dietary supplements

Vegan sources of calcium:
- dark leafy green vegetables
- pulses
- sesame seeds
- tahini
- fortified and unsweetened milk alternatives

Other food restrictions

Talk to your doctor and midwife if you:

- have coeliac disease or other food intolerances
- need to avoid food groups for cultural or religious reasons

They may need to refer you to a dietician to make sure your baby gets all the nutrients they need.

Feeling hungry?

During the 2nd and 3rd trimesters (from 14 weeks on), your body needs an extra 200 calories per day (kcal/day).

Here are examples of healthy snacks:

- fruit
- a yoghurt
- a small tin of salmon
- baked beans
- a glass of milk
- 20g almonds
- 2 rye crackers with light cheese
- 1 slice of bread with spread

From about 16 weeks onwards, I can taste traces of the food you eat in the amniotic fluid that I swallow.

Food safety

Food poisoning can be dangerous when you are pregnant, so take extra care when preparing food.

- Wash your hands before, during and after food preparation.
- Wash all fruits, vegetables and pre-packed salads very well before eating.
- Keep raw and cooked meats separate.
- Use different knives, chopping boards and other kitchen utensils when preparing raw and cooked meats to avoid cross-contamination.
- Put food in the fridge as quickly as possible. Eat leftovers within 2 to 3 days.
- Do not eat food that is past its 'use by' date.
- Make sure all meat, poultry, seafood and eggs are cooked thoroughly.

Foods to avoid during pregnancy

Foods to avoid	Reasons
✗ Unpasteurised dairy (milk and cheese)	Unpasteurised or mould-ripened products may contain harmful bacteria such as listeria. This can be dangerous for your baby
✗ Cheeses like brie and camembert	
✗ Soft blue cheeses such as Danish blue, gorgonzola and roquefort	
✗ Pâté	All types of pâté can contain listeria.
✗ Foods made with raw or undercooked eggs like homemade mayonnaise or mousse	To prevent salmonella food poisoning, which can cause severe vomiting and diarrhoea
✗ Raw or undercooked meat	To reduce the risk of toxoplasmosis. Although it's rare, it can be dangerous to developing babies
✗ Cold cured meats such as salami, Parma ham, chorizo and pepperoni	These meats are not cooked – they are just cured and fermented. This means there is a risk of toxoplasmosis
✗ Liver (including liver sausage, haggis and pâté containing liver)	Liver contains too much vitamin A, which can harm your baby
✗ Most fish is safe, but avoid shark, swordfish and marlin. Limit the amount of tuna you eat to 2 medium-sized cans of tuna per week	Shark, swordfish, marlin and too much tuna contain mercury. This could damage your baby's nervous system
✗ Don't have more than two portions of oily fish per week (like salmon, trout, mackerel, herring or fresh tuna)	Oily fish can contain pollutants such as dioxins
✗ Raw shellfish like clams, mussels or oysters	Can contain harmful viruses and bacteria
✗ Soft serve or soft whip ice-cream, like a '99'	To reduce the risk of listeria

Did you know?

- Peanuts are safe to eat during pregnancy if you are not allergic to them.
- White fish like cod and hake and cooked shellfish are safe to eat.
- All hard cheeses are safe to eat. For example, cheddar, edam, emmental and parmesan.
- Many soft cheeses such as cottage cheese, mozzarella, feta, goat's cheese are safe (providing they are made from pasteurised milk).

For more food safety information, go to safefood.eu

Tips for staying active

Physical activity in pregnancy is safe. It has lots of benefits for you and your baby.

Benefits for you

- Helps keep your weight gain under control.
- Helps you stay fit and prepare for the birth.
- Reduces your risk of pregnancy-related conditions like high blood pressure and gestational diabetes.
- Helps you sleep better.
- Improves your mood.
- May help you feel less tired.

Benefits for your baby

- Increased blood flow to the afterbirth (placenta).
- Reduces your baby's risk of complications from high blood pressure and gestational diabetes.

If you are new to exercise

- Start gradually and build it up.
- 10 minutes of walking is a good place to start.
- Every bout of 10 minutes you can do counts.
- Now is not the time to take up running.

If you are already active

- Keep going!
- Aim for 150 minutes of physical activity every week.
- Choose an exercise that makes you breathe faster.

Exercise safely

- Listen to your body – if it becomes uncomfortable, stop it.
- Use the 'talk test' – you will be breathing faster but you should still be able to hold a conversation. If not, slow down!
- Keep cool and wear loose clothing.
- Stay hydrated – drink plenty of water.

Other tips

- Choose an activity you enjoy.
- Involving your partner, family or friends can make exercise fun.
- Walking, swimming, using an exercise bike and low impact aerobics are all ideal exercises for pregnancy.

Mind the bump!

Some types of exercise are not safe when you are pregnant. These include:

- scuba diving
- any activity which might cause you to lose balance, such as horse-riding, skiing and gymnastics.
- lying flat on your back after 16 weeks – if lying on your back, elevate your head and upper back
- any sport where your bump could be bumped (like boxing, football or basketball)

Talk to your GP, obstetrician or midwife before starting an exercise programme if you:

- have any complications during your pregnancy like bleeding
- are carrying more than one baby

Looking for ideas to get your family active? See getirelandactive.ie

Exercises during pregnancy

Preparing your pelvic floor

The pelvic floor is a layer of muscles that runs from your pubic bone in front to your lower spine at the back.

What your pelvic muscles do

These muscles are shaped like a hammock. They support and hold your pelvic organs in place (uterus or womb, vagina, bowel, rectum and bladder).

Problems that can arise

The pelvic muscles come under a lot of strain during pregnancy and childbirth. If these muscles are weak, you may have problems with bladder or bowel control. Weak pelvic muscles could also mean your pelvic organs are less supported. This could lead to problems like pelvic organ prolapse.

How exercises help

Pelvic floor exercises help to strengthen these muscles.

In pregnancy, pelvic floor muscle training will help your body cope with the growing weight of the baby. Your muscles will mend more easily after the birth if they are healthy and fit before your baby is born.

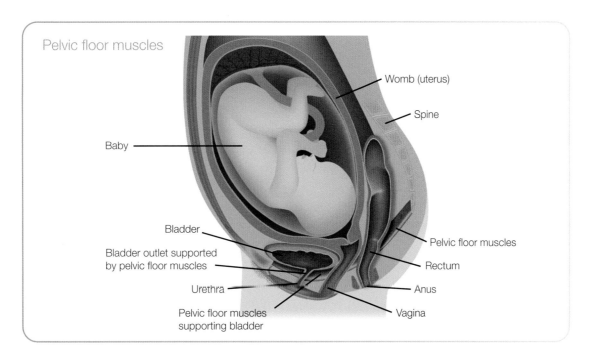

Pelvic floor muscles

- Womb (uterus)
- Spine
- Baby
- Bladder
- Bladder outlet supported by pelvic floor muscles
- Pelvic floor muscles
- Rectum
- Urethra
- Anus
- Pelvic floor muscles supporting bladder
- Vagina

How to do pelvic floor muscle exercises

These long and short exercises can be done anywhere at any time. You should try to do them three times each day.

Choose any comfortable position with the muscles of your thighs, bottom and stomach relaxed. Breathe normally while doing these exercises.

Exercise 1: Long pelvic floor squeezes

1. Tighten the muscles of your back passage as if you are holding in your wind.
2. At the same time, draw in your vagina as if you are trying to stop the flow of urine.
3. Once you can feel your pelvic floor muscles working, tighten them around your urethra (the tube between your bladder and the outside), your vagina and your back passage.
4. Hold for 3 to 5 seconds. If you can hold for up to 10 seconds, do so.
5. The squeeze must stay strong and you must feel a definite 'release' when you stop.
6. Repeat up to 10 times.

Exercise 2: Short pelvic floor squeezes

1. Squeeze and lift your pelvic floor muscles as quickly as possible.
2. Repeat this 10 times.

Exercise 3: Squeeze when you sneeze

As you breathe in to cough or sneeze, quickly tighten your pelvic floor muscles. Hold while you cough or sneeze. This is called 'the knack'.

Practice holding the muscle and coughing.

Urinary incontinence

Urinary incontinence (loss of bladder control) when exercising, coughing and sneezing is common in pregnancy. This is because your pelvic floor muscles become relaxed because of hormonal changes in pregnancy and increased pelvic pressure.

Talk to your GP or midwife about this. Ask them to refer you to a chartered physiotherapist who specialises in women's health if you have urinary incontinence.

Did you know?

Research shows that women who do pelvic floor exercises during their first pregnancy are less likely to have problems with bladder control (urinary incontinence) after the birth.

Back care

As your baby gets bigger, you may get back pain.

This exercise strengthens the tummy muscles that support your back:

1. Get on all fours.
2. Make sure your knees are under your hips and your elbows are under your shoulders. Your spine should be straight and in a neutral 'box' position.
3. Now arch your back towards the ceiling.
   Gently draw in your tummy muscles while breathing normally.
4. Return your back to the neutral position.
5. Repeat this 10 times.

Now is the time to develop good habits. Practice positions and techniques you might like to use during the birth of your baby. See page 118.

Thinking of using a birthing ball?

Sitting on a birthing ball can be a comfortable position when you need to rest. Rocking back and forth can be soothing.

In early labour, sitting on a birthing ball can help gravity to stretch your cervix.

Practice

If you think you would like to use a birthing ball during the birth, practice sitting on it at home during your pregnancy.

Anti-burst

If buying one, choose a professional quality anti-burst ball.

Hips higher than knees

Make sure the ball is inflated so that your hips are higher than your knees.

Pelvic girdle pain

Pelvic girdle pain (PGP) is the term given to pain in the joints that make up your pelvic girdle. It can cause pain in pubic bone, thighs, groin and lower back.

It can affect up to 1 in 5 women during their pregnancy. Pain can vary from mild to severe.

Tips to help with pelvic girdle pain and back pain:

Things to avoid:

- standing to do tasks that can be done while sitting
- standing on one leg when you are getting dressed and undressed
- lifting heavy objects

Posture

- Stand tall by lengthening up through the crown of your head to keep the pelvic floor and core muscles active to support baby, pelvis and spine.
- Sit tall. Don't slump and support your back with a small cushion.

- Draw in your abdominal muscles around your baby during all daily activities, especially when you are walking or lifting.
- Work at a surface high enough to prevent you stooping.
- Try to balance the weight between two bags when carrying shopping.

Shoes

- Wear flat shoes or supportive footwear as these allow your weight to be evenly distributed.

Rest

- Make sure you get enough rest, particularly later in pregnancy.

Pregnancy yoga or pilates can help improve your posture, physical health and wellbeing.

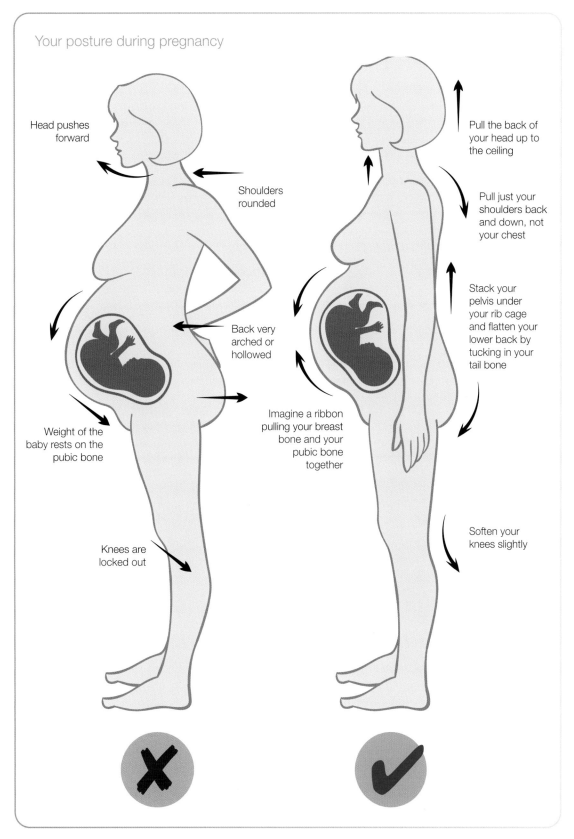

Your posture during pregnancy

Head pushes forward

Shoulders rounded

Back very arched or hollowed

Weight of the baby rests on the pubic bone

Imagine a ribbon pulling your breast bone and your pubic bone together

Knees are locked out

Pull the back of your head up to the ceiling

Pull just your shoulders back and down, not your chest

Stack your pelvis under your rib cage and flatten your lower back by tucking in your tail bone

Soften your knees slightly

Contact your GP, midwife or physiotherapist if your symptoms do not improve within a few weeks or interfere with your normal activities.

Sex during pregnancy

It is safe to have sex when you are pregnant. Most women with no pregnancy complications are able to continue having sex right up until their due date.

You may notice that there are changes in your sexual desires. As your pregnancy advances, some positions may become uncomfortable.

Positions

For example, sex with your partner on top can become uncomfortable quite early in pregnancy. It may be better to lie on your sides, either facing each other or with your partner behind. Explore comfortable activities that work for both of you.

Will having sex harm the baby?

You cannot hurt your baby by having sex. The baby is protected by the amniotic sac (the balloon of water around the baby) which acts as a shock absorber. There is a thick mucus plug at the neck of your womb (cervix) that will also protect the baby.

If you are having sex with a male partner, the penis does not go further than the vagina. It cannot reach your baby.

Sex in pregnancy is safe for most women. However, you may be advised to avoid sex if you have:

- any heavy bleeding
- a low-lying placenta
- haematoma

Speak to your midwife or your GP if you are not sure.

Sexually transmitted infections (STIs)

Sexually transmitted infections (STIs) can be dangerous for your baby. Always use a condom if:

- you are having sex with a casual partner
- you or your partner have other partners
- your regular partner has any symptoms of STIs, such as discharge from or blistering on his penis

Myth busters

Some women have sex late in their pregnancy because they believe it will make them go into labour sooner. There is no evidence to support that belief. However, neither you nor your baby will be harmed if your pregnancy is normal and you decide to have sex.

Healthy pregnancy weight gain

Healthy weight gain during pregnancy helps your:

- uterus (womb) and placenta (afterbirth) to grow
- baby to grow
- body to prepare for breastfeeding
- blood volume to increase and supply your baby with oxygen and nutrients

Benefits for you	Benefits for your baby
Feel healthier and have more energy	Lower risk of complications at birth
Gets you to healthier weight more quickly after the baby is born	More likely to be born at a healthy weight
Reduces your risk of complications during pregnancy and birth	Less risk of medical problems such as diabetes in later life

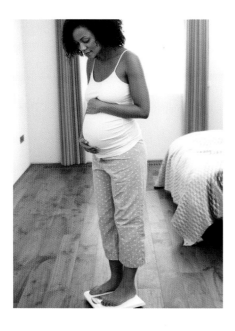

What is a healthy weight gain during pregnancy?

Most of the weight gain during your pregnancy happens in the second and third trimesters.

Eat 'twice as healthy', not 'twice as much'.

Your body mass index (BMI)

A healthy pregnancy weight gain depends on your Body Mass Index (BMI) before you became pregnant. Your BMI is a measure of your weight in relation to your height. Your GP or midwife can work this out for you.

A healthy BMI is above 18.5 but less than 25.

There is a BMI calculator on safefood.eu

How much weight you should gain during pregnancy:	
Healthy weight	an average of 0.5 kg (1 pound) per week
Overweight	an average of 0.27 kg (just over half a pound) per week
Obese	an average of 0.22 kg (just under half a pound) per week
Underweight	may be advised to gain more than 0.5 kg (1 pound) per week

If you are underweight

If you are underweight or have a low BMI in pregnancy, you have an increased chance of:

- premature birth
- your baby being small and having a low birth weight
- anaemia - this is when there are not enough healthy red blood cells to carry oxygen around your body

Your midwife, GP or obstetrician will monitor your weight. They may refer you to a dietitian.

Worried you may be overweight or obese?

Risks

Being overweight or obese during pregnancy increases your risk of complications like:

- gestational diabetes – high blood sugar that develops during the pregnancy and usually disappears after birth (see page 90)
- high blood pressure

There are also some risks to your baby, including excessive birth weight. They may be born with low blood sugars or breathing problems.

What you can do

Talk to your GP, midwife or obstetrician about ways to reduce the risk to you and your baby. They may advise you to increase your dose of folic acid and take vitamin D supplements. You might need extra ultrasound scans if your BMI is over 30.

You should also discuss with your obstetrician or midwife the safest way and place for you to give birth.

Losing weight is never recommended when you are pregnant. However, by making healthy changes to the way you eat during pregnancy, you may reduce the amount of weight that you gain. This is not harmful. Exercise safely.

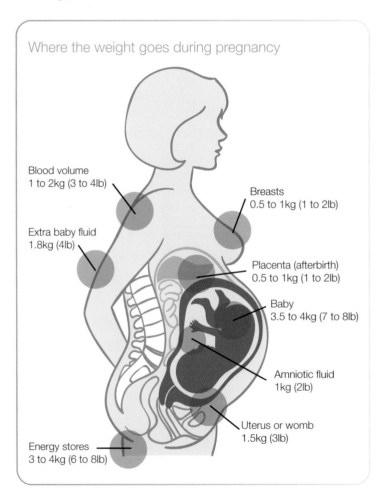

Where the weight goes during pregnancy

Blood volume
1 to 2kg (3 to 4lb)

Breasts
0.5 to 1kg (1 to 2lb)

Extra baby fluid
1.8kg (4lb)

Placenta (afterbirth)
0.5 to 1kg (1 to 2lb)

Baby
3.5 to 4kg (7 to 8lb)

Amniotic fluid
1kg (2lb)

Uterus or womb
1.5kg (3lb)

Energy stores
3 to 4kg (6 to 8lb)

Alcohol and pregnancy

It is best to not drink alcohol at all if you are pregnant. Alcohol can damage your baby's developing brain and body.

Drinking while pregnant doesn't mean your baby will definitely be harmed, but it can happen. The effects may not be evident at birth.

Alcohol passes from the mother's blood into the baby's blood through the placenta. The placenta does not act as a barrier to alcohol.

How alcohol causes harm

Drinking alcohol while pregnant can cause:

- miscarriage
- your baby being born premature or with a low birth weight
- foetal alcohol spectrum disorders (FASD)
- foetal alcohol syndrome (FAS)

Foetal alcohol spectrum disorders (FASD)

FASD causes problems with a baby's body, brain, behaviour and can cause problems throughout a person's life.

For example:

- hyperactivity and poor attention
- learning difficulties and a lower IQ
- difficulty getting along with other people
- being smaller than expected
- problems with eating and sleeping
- emotional and mental health problems

Foetal alcohol syndrome (FAS)

Foetal alcohol syndrome (FAS) is more serious. It can happen when you drink heavily during your pregnancy at levels that exceed low risk alcohol use guidelines. In addition to all the signs of FASD listed above, your baby may:

- be smaller than normal or underweight
- have damage to their brain and spinal cord
- have an abnormally small head or eyes, abnormally-shaped ears or facial features
- have problems with their heart or other organs

Drinking alcohol at any time can cause damage. This is because your baby's brain develops throughout pregnancy.

Drinking, especially drinking in excess of low risk guidelines during the first three months of pregnancy, is particularly harmful. This is the time when your baby's body organs and facial features are developing.

Will the occasional drink do any harm?

- There is no proven level of safe drinking during pregnancy.
- Heavy or frequent drinking is particularly dangerous.
- The safest thing you can do is not to drink alcohol at all during pregnancy.

What if I have already drunk alcohol during my pregnancy?

Stop drinking alcohol for the rest of your pregnancy. The less your baby is exposed to alcohol over the course of the pregnancy, the greater their chance for healthy brain growth and development. Try not to worry. The main thing is that you stop now.

How others can help

Your partner, family and friends can help by:

- avoiding drinking alcohol around you
- taking part in social activities with you that don't revolve around alcohol
- helping you reduce the stress in your life

For more information and help to stop drinking alcohol, you can:

- talk to your GP, obstetrician or midwife
- visit askaboutalcohol.ie
- call the HSE Alcohol and Drugs Helpline for free on 1800 459 459 and speak in confidence with a professional

Smoking during pregnancy

If you are pregnant and you smoke, the best thing you can do for your baby is to stop. Quitting smoking can be difficult, so ask for help.

The earlier you stop, the greater the benefits. Stopping completely is the only effective way to protect yourself and your baby. It's never too late.

Smoking when pregnant is harmful to you and your baby. Inhaling smoke from other people's cigarettes (passive smoking) can also harm your baby.

Smoking cuts down the amount of oxygen and nutrients that get to your baby through the placenta. As soon as you stop, the chemicals will start to clear from your body and your baby will get more oxygen.

Benefits of quitting for you and your baby

If you smoke, stopping during pregnancy will reduce these risks:

- miscarriage
- ectopic pregnancy
- bleeding during pregnancy
- placenta complications
- your baby growing too slowly in the womb
- stillbirth
- premature birth

- your baby dying shortly after birth
- cot death (sudden infant death syndrome)
- birth defects
- low birth weight
- asthma, ear infections and pneumonia

What you can do

Cutting down is a positive step, but stopping completely is better for your baby.

- Ask for help to quit smoking.
- Ask friends and family not to smoke around you when you are pregnant or around the baby after they are born.
- Your partner, family and friends can encourage you by stopping smoking too.
- Make your home and car smoke-free areas.

For help to stop smoking:

- Visit quit.ie, freephone 1800 201 203 or freetext QUIT to 50100 for free advice and support to quit smoking.
- Talk to your GP, obstetrician or midwife - they may refer you to a smoking cessation clinic.
- Some maternity hospitals have trained smoking cessation midwives.

Nicotine replacement therapy

Nicotine replacement therapy can reduce or remove the physical symptoms of withdrawal. Talk to your smoking cessation practitioner, GP, midwife, pharmacist or obstetrician before using it during pregnancy.

E-cigarettes

E-cigarettes are not safe or effective in helping to quit smoking in pregnancy. They are not currently recommended for pregnant women.

Myth-busters

Sometimes people joke that a benefit to smoking in pregnancy is a smaller baby. However, a baby that is small due to smoking is not a healthy baby.

Drugs and chemicals

Medications

Let your GP, obstetrician or midwife know if you are taking any medication during the pregnancy. This includes:

- prescribed medications
- over the counter medications
- supplements

Review all prescription medications with them. In general, you should avoid taking medications when pregnant. You might need to keep taking certain medications while others may be stopped.

Over-the-counter medication and herbal supplements

Many over-the counter-medications (no prescription needed) or herbal supplements may not be safe during pregnancy.

Breastfeeding

Some medications that are unsafe during pregnancy are safe to take while breastfeeding. Ask your GP or pharmacist for advice.

Illegal, recreational or 'street' drugs

Do not be afraid to tell your healthcare team if you are using drugs. Your midwives and doctors are there to support you, they will not judge you.

You may be offered substitute medication to reduce your drug use and stabilise you. You and your baby are less likely to become ill if your doctor and midwife know.

It is not safe to take the following drugs during pregnancy:

- marijuana
- crack or cocaine
- crystal meth
- ecstasy
- LSD
- heroin

Taking these drugs could harm you or your baby. If you are using drugs, the sooner you get advice the better. Talk to your GP.

> **Babies born to mothers who take drugs may:**
> - be born too early or too small
> - have birth defects or medical problems
> - have problems learning
> - go through drug withdrawal

Heroin

If you are using heroin, do not stop this suddenly. Get advice from your GP immediately.

Benzodiazepines

Benzodiazepines are sometimes called benzos. If you are using benzodiazepines, do not stop these suddenly. These should be reduced gradually during the pregnancy.

Cocaine

Cocaine can be stopped suddenly.

> ## Methadone
> Reducing methadone doses during pregnancy is possible but needs to be done under medical supervision. This is because there is a risk of miscarriage, premature birth and relapse.

> ## To get help
> - Call the HSE Drugs Helpline on 1800 459 459.
> - Go to drugs.ie
> - Talk to your GP, obstetrician or midwife.

Caffeine

Too much caffeine is not good for your unborn baby. High levels of caffeine can cause your baby to have a low birth weight. It can also increase the chance of miscarriage.

High caffeine levels during pregnancy can increase your blood pressure, and may cause dehydration.

What foods and drinks contain caffeine?
- coffee
- tea
- chocolate
- soft drinks
- energy drinks
- some herbal teas like green tea

There's not much information available about which herbal teas are safe to drink during pregnancy. To be safe, do not drink more than 4 cups of herbal tea each day. Be aware of caffeine in green tea. If you are not sure about a herbal tea, talk to your midwife or GP before drinking it.

Limit to 200mg a day

You can have up to 200mg of caffeine a day.

Food or drink	Amount of caffeine
1 mug tea	75 mg
1 mug instant coffee	100mg
1 mug filter coffee	140mg
1 can cola or diet cola	40mg
1 energy drink	60mg
1 x 50g bar of milk chocolate	25mg
1 x 50mg bar of plain or dark chocolate	50 mg

200mg of caffeine is:

- 2 mugs of instant coffee
- less than 3 cups of tea
- 1 cup of filter coffee and a bar of plain chocolate

Going out for coffee?

Many of us love popping to a café for a cup of coffee. However, caffeine levels can vary between coffee shops from 80 to 300mg per cup.

Water is the best drink

Water is the best thing to drink when you are thirsty. Try adding slices of lemon or fresh fruit, a sprig of mint or cucumber to make it more exciting.

Before you knew were pregnant

You may have consumed, used or abused a harmful substance before you realised you were pregnant. This might include alcohol, medication, drugs or cigarettes. You may be worried about this.

Remember:

- You are a caring mother and doing the best you can.
- You cannot change the past, but you can change the present. You can make positive changes for your baby and yourself.
- Over 97% of babies are born well and healthy.
- Ignore suggestions from others that you are to blame if something goes wrong.
- Try to escape the guilt – talk to your partner, a trusted friend or a professional like your GP or midwife.

Even when problems do occur, it is usually not due to an isolated incident or a few doses of medication.

Working during pregnancy

Most jobs are safe to continue while pregnant. After all, pregnancy is not an illness and most people feel well throughout their pregnancies.

In most jobs, simply making small changes will help you have a healthy pregnancy and be more comfortable at work.

However, some women must tell their employers as soon as they discover they are pregnant. This is because the type of work that they do is unsuitable for pregnant women.

Regulations

The Safety, Health and Welfare at Work (General Application) Regulations 2007, Part 6, Chapter 2, Protection of Pregnant, Post Natal and Breastfeeding Employees (The Pregnancy at Work Regulations) apply.

These state that employers must do all they can to ensure your safety and health when you are pregnant or breastfeeding.

Risks to pregnant workers

Tell your GP, midwife or obstetrician if you are in contact with:

- x-rays
- lead
- pesticides
- mercury
- asbestos
- plastics
- extreme heat, for example, saunas
- some cleaning products or solvents

Practical aspects

It is advisable to reduce the following activities, particularly in the later stages of pregnancy:

- hard physical work
- lifting heavy loads
- prolonged standing for more than 3 hours at a time
- long working hours

Night shifts

There is no evidence that working night shifts is more harmful when you are pregnant. However, your GP or obstetrician may say that it is necessary for your safety or health to stop. If so, your employer will need to make alternative arrangements.

Coping with work while pregnant

You may feel exhausted, particularly at the start or towards the end of the pregnancy. Things that may help include:

- Use your lunch-break to eat and rest, not for running errands.

- Don't rush home from work and do another day's work at home. Get help with household chores, try to keep housework to a minimum and get to bed early.

- Ask your partner or family and friends to help with other children when you get home.

Maternity benefit

Most employed and self-employed women are entitled to receive maternity benefit payments.

You should apply for the payment 6 weeks before going on leave (12 weeks if you are self-employed).

For more information, search for 'maternity benefit' on citizensinformation.ie

Paternity leave and benefit

Not forgetting fathers, co-habiting partners or spouses! The Paternity Leave and Benefit Act 2016 means fathers are entitled to statutory paternity leave of 2 weeks.

Travelling while pregnant

Road travel

Road traffic collisions are one of the most common causes of injury to pregnant women. If you are in a road traffic accident, always get advice from your maternity unit or hospital or your GP.

Correct seatbelt position

To protect you and your baby, always wear your seatbelt. The safest way for pregnant women to wear a seatbelt is to:

- Place the diagonal section of the belt across your chest area with the strap resting on your shoulder, not your neck.
- Place the lap section of the belt flat on thighs, not over your bump.

Wear your seatbelt as tightly as possible to keep you and your baby safe.

'Lap only' seatbelts

Avoid 'lap only' seatbelts when pregnant. These can cause serious injuries to your unborn baby if the car driver brakes suddenly or you are in a collision.

> For more information on safe seatbelt use in pregnancy, visit rsa.ie

Air travel

If your pregnancy is straightforward, flying is not harmful to you or to your baby. Flying does not increase your risk of early labour or miscarriage.

When to fly

You are safe to fly up to 37 weeks if you're pregnant with one baby. You can fly up to 32 weeks if you're expecting twins or a multiple birth. Check with your airline before you book.

Radiation

Anyone who flies is exposed to a slight increase in radiation. Occasional flights do not put you or your baby at risk.

If you are a member of a flight crew or you fly regularly as part of your job, speak to your manager or occupational health department about your situation.

Should I expect any problems if I fly?

- Blocked nose and ears – during pregnancy you are more likely to have a blocked nose, this may worsen while travelling.
- Swelling of your legs may worsen during a flight.
- If you have pregnancy sickness or morning sickness already, the motion of the flight may worsen this.

DVT (deep vein thrombosis)

A DVT is a blood clot that can form in your leg. If it travels to your lungs it can be dangerous. Your risk of DVT increases during pregnancy and for 6 weeks after birth.

Short-haul flights (less than 4 hours)

If you are taking a short-haul flight (less than 4 hours), no special measures are necessary.

Long haul flights (longer than 4 hours)

- Wear loose clothing and comfy shoes.
- Take regular walks and do in-seat exercises.
- Drink plenty of water.
- Wear graduated elastic compression stockings – your midwife, GP or pharmacist will need to measure you for these.

If you have other risk factors, your GP might recommend an injection of a blood thinner such as low molecular weight heparin.

Before you go

Before you travel, think about where you're going:

- Do you need travel vaccines?
- Could you access medical care easily if you need it?
- In the unlikely event of premature labour, is there a maternity hospital close to your destination? Are there facilities for premature babies?

European health insurance card

If you're travelling to Europe, make sure to get a European health insurance card. It is free and allows you to get free access to health services in other EU countries.

For information, search 'European health insurance card' on HSE.ie

Don't forget to bring

- any medications, including your folic acid
- a letter from your GP or obstetrician
- your medical notes if you normally carry them – if not, bring your antenatal care card

The letter from your GP or obstetrician should state:

- that you are pregnant
- how many weeks you are
- that you have no pregnancy complications (if this is the case)

Flying may not be recommended if you:

- have certain medical conditions such as severe anaemia
- are at risk of premature labour
- have had a heavy bleed

Domestic violence or abuse

Domestic violence is any behaviour within your close relationships that makes you feel:

- scared
- isolated from your family or friends
- threatens your safety and wellbeing

Domestic violence is abuse that happens in close, intimate or family relationships. It can be physical, emotional, sexual, financial or mental.

Domestic abuse can change during pregnancy. It can also get worse and become more dangerous. Being pregnant does not protect you from domestic violence.

Remember, domestic violence is never acceptable. It is not your fault.

Warning signs

An abuser can use a range of behaviours and actions to get power and control over their partner. It is important for you and your baby to recognise when you might be at risk or in danger.

Signs of an abusive relationship with a current or ex-partner can include any of the following. You:

- feel afraid
- feel controlled
- have been hurt or injured
- have been forced to do things you don't want to do

Dangers during and after pregnancy

Any form of abuse during pregnancy can be very dangerous. Pregnancy or just after having a baby is known as a high risk time for women in abusive relationships.

It can lead to death of you or your baby, injuries and mental health problems.

Experiencing domestic violence means you are more likely to have:

- a premature birth
- a low birth weight baby
- poor weight gain during pregnancy
- infections
- other serious pregnancy health complications

Women in Ireland also report having miscarriages because of physical violence during pregnancy.

Where to get help and information

The first step to protect yourself is to talk to somebody you trust. This could be a friend, family member or a domestic violence support service.

Help, supports and safe accommodation are available to all women in Ireland. This includes women who are pregnant, have a baby or have had a miscarriage.

Who to contact

- If in immediate danger, call the Gardaí on 999 or 112. Find your local Garda station at garda.ie
- Talk to your GP, midwife, GP practice nurse or public health nurse.
- Women's Aid: free and confidential support (24 hours a day), freephone 1800 341 900 or visit womensaid.ie
- Safe Ireland: information on women's refuges and supports, see safeireland.ie
- Rape Crisis Centres offer free and confidential support 24 hours a day, freephone 1800 77 8888 or visit rapecrisishelp.ie
- Sexual assault treatment units: details at hse.ie/satu

Cosc is the National Office for Prevention of Domestic, Sexual and Gender-based Violence. Their website has information on domestic violence support services near you.

It has also advice on digital safety. This is useful if you are concerned your partner is monitoring your internet searches.

whatwouldyoudo.ie

Did you know?

Your midwife will usually ask to see you alone, at least once. This is to give you an opportunity to tell them about concerns or worries you might prefer your partner not to hear. Talk to your midwife if you think you are experiencing domestic violence.

Female genital mutilation

Female genital mutilation (FGM) is also known as female circumcision or cutting. FGM is the harming, injuring, cutting or removal of part or all female external genitalia for no medical reason.

It can cause serious harm to girls and women and leave them with ongoing health problems for all of their lives. It is estimated that over 5,000 women living in Ireland have undergone FGM before they moved here.

Complications in pregnancy, labour and birth

FGM can cause complications and problems before and during pregnancy. It can also make labour and giving birth difficult.

If you have had FGM

If you have had FGM, you should talk to your GP, midwife or obstetrician as early as possible in your pregnancy.

This means you can:

- take care of your health during your pregnancy
- plan the safest method of delivering your baby

FGM supports

FGM treatment service

The HSE supports a free FGM treatment service. This is at the Irish Family Planning Association (IFPA) in Dublin city centre.

Women and girls in Ireland who have had FGM can receive free medical, psychological, sexual and reproductive health care.

Anyone living anywhere in Ireland can make an appointment. You do not need your doctor or GP to refer you.

Address:

FGM Treatment Service, 5/7 Cathal Brugha Street, Dublin 1
Phone number: 01 872 7088.
FGM Treatment Service confidential phone line: 085 877 1342

Akidwa

Akidwa is an organisation that provides support to women living with FGM. Contact Akidwa at 01-834 9851, visit akidwa.ie or email info@akidwa.ie

Infections during pregnancy

Every day we come into contact with many germs, such as viruses and bacteria that could cause infection.

Normally our immune system deals with these germs. When you are pregnant, your body naturally weakens your immune system. This is to help your pregnancy continue successfully. It means that when you are pregnant, some infections can be dangerous for you and your baby.

It is important to speak to your GP, obstetrician or midwife if you think you have an infection as occasionally you may need to take medicine.

Prevention

Think about the ways you can avoid infections, like being careful when washing your hands and preparing food. Getting certain vaccines (page 66) can protect you and your baby.

Types in pregnancy

Some of the infections that can cause problems for pregnant women include urine (kidney or bladder) and vaginal infections such as:

- urinary tract infection (UTI)
- bacterial vaginosis (BV)
- group B strep (GBS)
- sexually transmitted diseases (STIs)

Urinary tract infection (UTI)

This is an infection in the bladder. You may have pain on passing urine (when you do a wee).

It can also cause:

- the need to pass urine more frequently
- a high temperature
- lower back pain

If this UTI not treated, it can cause early labour.

If you develop any of these symptoms, see your GP or midwife. Drink plenty of fluids. Always wipe from front to back after passing urine or when cleaning your genital area so as to stop germs from spreading from your bum to your bladder.

Bacterial vaginosis (BV)

BV causes a vaginal discharge. It may be white or grey in colour and may smell fishy.

If BV is not treated, it can cause:

- early labour
- miscarriage
- infection of the uterus (womb) after childbirth

Do not:

✗ push water into your vagina to clean it (douching)

✗ wash around your vagina too often – once a day is enough

If you had BV in the past, do not add bath oils, detergents, bubble bath or similar products to bath water. Tell your GP, obstetrician or midwife if you develop unusual vaginal discharge.

Group B strep (GBS)

Group B strep (GBS) is a germ carried by many people in the vagina. There are usually no symptoms. The germ can be detected on a urine sample or a vaginal swab. If you test positive, this is called 'carrying' GBS.

Effect on baby

If you are carrying GBS, there is a small chance that you could pass this to your baby during the birth. If this happens, your baby could develop GBS infection. GBS infection can make your baby ill.

It can also cause serious complications such as pneumonia, meningitis or septicaemia (severe infection of the blood stream).

Antibiotics

If you test positive for this germ, you will be offered antibiotics during labour. These are usually given through a drip in your arm.

Sexually transmitted infections (STIs)

STIs are a group of infections that can be passed from person to person during sex.

These infections include:

- chlamydia
- gonorrhoea
- syphilis
- genital herpes
- genital warts
- HIV
- hepatitis B and C

Symptoms

Many STIs do not have symptoms. Some can cause abnormal vaginal discharge, or rashes or blisters on the genitals.

Effect on baby

Some STIs can affect your baby's health during pregnancy and after birth.

Get checked

If you have any reason to believe that you or your partner has an STI, you should go for a check-up as soon as you can.

Hepatitis B and HIV

If you have hepatitis B or HIV, you and your baby can be treated to prevent your baby from becoming ill.

> If you have any reason to believe that you or your partner has an STI, go for a check-up as soon as you can.
>
> Ask your GP or midwife, or go to a sexual health clinic. Find sexual health services on sexualwellbeing.ie

Some infections are more obvious and may cause you to feel unwell or have a rash.

These are:

- chickenpox
- Parvovirus B19 ('slapped cheek')

Chickenpox

Chickenpox is an infectious illness caused by a virus called varicella zoster. Over 90% of pregnant women are immune to chickenpox. For those who are not immune, it can cause:

- fever
- feeling unwell
- an itchy rash

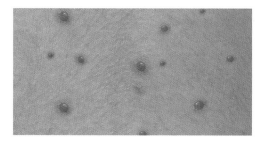

Dangers

Chickenpox can be dangerous for mothers and babies.

What to do

Contact your GP, obstetrician or midwife immediately if you:

- suspect you have chickenpox
- come into contact with chickenpox and you have not had it before

Your obstetrician and midwife will offer you treatments to reduce the risk to you and your baby.

Parvovirus B19 'slapped cheek'

Parvovirus is a viral infection that is very common in children. This virus may cause a red rash on the face like a 'slapped cheek'.

Effect on baby

Most pregnant women are immune to parvovirus. In most cases, the baby is not affected if the pregnant mother gets the virus.

In rare cases, parvovirus can cause the baby to be anaemic. This is dangerous if untreated.

What to do

If you come into contact with parvovirus, contact your GP, obstetrician or midwife.

Some infections are not obvious and you may have no symptoms. Many of these infections come from food or animals. It is very important to protect yourself from these infections as they can make your baby ill. These are:

- toxoplasmosis
- listeria
- hepatitis E

Toxoplasmosis

Toxoplasmosis is an infection that you can get from:

- eating raw or undercooked meat
- infected cat poo
- eating unwashed vegetables
- being in contact with lambs and sheep during lambing season

It often has no symptoms but it can make your baby very unwell. If you feel you may be at risk, talk to your doctor or midwife as there are treatments available.

Toxoplasmosis (continued)

Prevention

To prevent toxoplasmosis:

- cook meat well
- wash vegetables well
- wash your hands and all surfaces before and after preparing food
- do not eat or drink unpasteurised dairy products
- get someone else to change the cat litter tray each day

If you can't get somebody to deal with cat poo for you, then make sure you wear gloves, use a scoop to remove the poo and wash your hands well after. Always wear gloves if you are gardening or handling soil, and wash your hands well afterwards.

Listeria

This is an infection you can get from eating food contaminated with the listeria germ.

It can cause:

- fever
- vomiting
- diarrhoea
- pregnancy and birth complications, including stillbirth

What to do

If you think you have listeria, tell your GP, obstetrician or midwife immediately.

Prevention

To prevent listeria infection:

- avoid eating soft or mould-ripened cheeses like brie, camembert and Danish blue
- never eat foods past the 'use by' date
- cook food thoroughly
- store food properly, for example using your fridge and sealed containers

Hepatitis E

Pigs can be a source of hepatitis E infection.

This is dangerous for pregnant women so avoid contact with pigs and pig faeces.

Vaccines during pregnancy

You should vaccinate your baby after birth to protect them from serious diseases. (See page 191). But did you know there are two safe and effective vaccines you can get during pregnancy to protect you and your baby?

These are the:

- whooping cough vaccine (pertussis)
- flu vaccine

Whooping cough vaccine

What is whooping cough?	Whooping cough (pertussis) is a highly contagious illness caused by the germ Bordetella pertussis.
Why is whooping cough dangerous?	The levels of whooping cough in Ireland are increasing and babies who are too young to be vaccinated are at greatest risk.
	Young babies with whooping cough can become very ill and are most likely to be admitted to hospital. Young babies are also at risk of developing a severe case of whooping cough, which can cause death.
What can I do?	You can protect your baby by getting vaccinated any time from 16 weeks up to 36 weeks. You can still be vaccinated up to 36 weeks but this may not be as effective as getting it earlier on.
Is the vaccine safe?	Yes. The vaccine is widely used in the UK, Australia, the US and New Zealand with no reported safety concerns. A large study in the UK of over 20,000 women found no evidence of risks to pregnancy or babies.
What are the side effects of the vaccine?	The side effects are mild. You may get soreness or redness around the injection site. You may get mild fever and fatigue for up to 48 hours after you get the vaccine.
If I can't get the vaccine or my baby comes early?	Make sure all your other children are vaccinated. Ask relatives and friends not to visit if they have a cough. If your baby is premature, make sure all adults in the house get the whooping cough vaccine.

"If you are a stranger or if you have a cough, no kisses!"

Flu vaccine

Why do I need the flu vaccine?	If you are pregnant and get the flu, you have a higher chance of: • becoming seriously unwell • developing complications like pneumonia, meningitis or encephalitis
Will the vaccine protect my baby?	Yes. If you get the flu, your baby could be born prematurely or could even die. Vaccination could protect your baby for up to 6 months after the birth.
Will the vaccine give me the flu?	No. The flu vaccine contains killed viruses. This means it cannot cause the flu.
Is the vaccine safe?	Yes, the flu vaccine has been given to millions of pregnant women. It has been used in the United States for over 60 years.
Can I get the flu vaccine at the same time as the whooping cough vaccine?	Yes.

Other vaccines during pregnancy

It is safe to have many vaccines, such as a tetanus shot, while you are pregnant.

However, some vaccines are not safe to receive while pregnant. Particularly 'live' vaccines such as the yellow fever vaccine or the measles, mumps and rubella vaccine (MMR).

When you book in for vaccines, always tell your doctor or pharmacist if you think you may be pregnant.

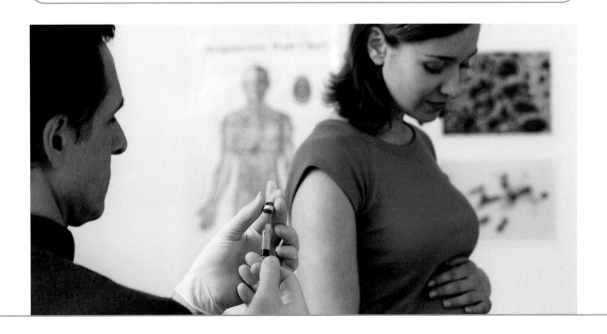

Your pregnancy week by week

Week 0 to 13: The first trimester

Week 8

Their eyes develop. Their heart is beating twice as fast as yours.

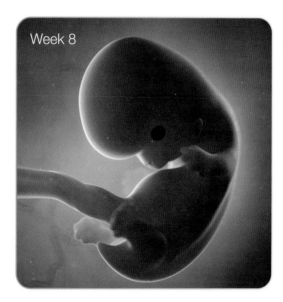

Week 8

Week 9

Tiny toes form. The brain is growing.

Week 10

The neck begins to develop.

Week 11

Boy or girl? The genitalia are developing. Taste buds are developing.

Week 12

Almost all of the organs and structures have formed. These will continue to grow until they are born.

Week 13

They are about 7 to 10 cm long – about the size of a peapod. They now have fingernails and toenails.

They can:

- move their arms and legs, although you probably won't feel it yet
- suck their thumb

The following are forming and developing:

- face (the eyes are closed)
- fingerprints
- vocal cords
- digestive system
- pancreas
- bones
- brain
- spine

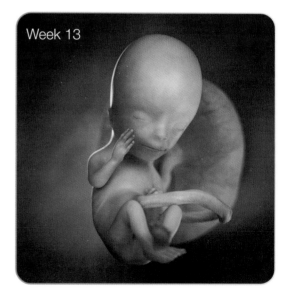

Week 13

Week 0 to 13: changes you may feel

Mood swings

Mood swings in pregnancy are very common. They are caused by:

- hormonal changes
- feeling unwell
- being more tired
- any stress or anxiety that you may be feeling

What to do

- Talk to someone! A trusted friend, your partner or your family.
- You may have less interest in sex or usual activities, especially if you feel sick.
- If these feelings are very intense or severe, talk to your GP, obstetrician or midwife.

Tiredness

Growing a baby is hard work! Hormonal changes can cause tiredness.

What to do

- Rest when you can and get a good night's sleep.
- Ask for help and accept offers of help.
- Drink lots of fluids (2 litres per day).
- Eat small meals often.
- Take regular exercise.

Morning sickness

Morning sickness is a combination of nausea and vomiting. It can happen at any time of day. The most likely cause is the hormonal changes that take place during pregnancy. It usually settles by 20 weeks.

What to do

- Have crackers beside the bed and eat them before you get up.
- Get up slowly.
- Eat small amounts every 1 to 2 hours.
- Eat bland food.
- Drink plenty of water (aim for 10 to 12 cups each day).

Go to your GP, obstetrician or midwife if:

- your nausea and vomiting is severe
- you are not keeping water down (you vomit soon after drinking it)

If you vomit, rinse your mouth out with water. Your teeth will be softened by your stomach acid so do not brush straight away. Wait about an hour.

Vaginal discharge

This is clear or white fluid that may come out of your vagina.

What to do

- Wear loose cotton underwear.
- Don't overclean or douche (push water into your vagina to clean it).

> Contact your GP or midwife if:
>
> - the discharge changes colour, especially if it's green, brown or yellow
> - you notice an unpleasant smell
> - you feel itchy or sore, or
> - you notice any blood in the discharge

Passing urine more often

> This is caused by:
>
> - hormonal changes
> - increased fluid levels
> - added pressure from the growing baby on your bladder

What to do

- Even though frequent trips to the bathroom are annoying, keep drinking plenty of fluids. This is very important for you and your baby.
- Cut back on drinks containing caffeine like tea, coffee and energy drinks.
- Make sure your bladder empties fully each time you pee.
- Do your pelvic floor exercises (see page 39).

If you are passing urine often or leaking urine, speak to your GP, obstetrician or midwife who can refer you to see a physiotherapist.

Breasts getting bigger

This is your body's way of preparing for breastfeeding.

What to do

- Wear a supportive bra.
- Avoid bras with underwire.

Dizziness

This is caused by:

- increasing demands on your circulatory system
- changing hormone levels

What to do
- Get up slowly.
- After waking, sit on the side of the bed before you get up.
- Eat small regular meals and drink plenty of fluids.

Emotional changes

You may feel a range of emotions. These could include anxiety about the future or ambivalence (not sure if you want to be pregnant).

What to do

During these times it is very important to have your feelings understood and supported.

Feelings you may have

You may notice a range of feelings during the first trimester. You might be overjoyed, terrified or somewhere in between. You might feel anxious. You might feel ambivalence (not entirely sure you want to be a parent).

It is normal to wonder "do I want to be a parent?" as you think about the responsibilities of caring for your baby. It is common for fathers and partners to have these feelings too.

You may have feelings of fear and anxiety if you:
- conceived by IVF
- had a previous pregnancy loss

What to do

Talking to your partner, support person, family or friends can help you to deal with these feelings.

If these feelings are very intense or severe, talk to your GP, midwife or obstetrician.

If you are pregnant but not sure you want to be, you can talk to your GP or a HSE-funded unplanned pregnancy counselling service. Visit myoptions.ie or freephone 1800 828 010 for information.

Contact your GP or maternity unit or hospital urgently if you have vaginal bleeding or severe abdominal pain.

Miscarriage

The word 'miscarriage' describes the loss of a pregnancy before 24 weeks. Sadly, at least one in five pregnancies ends in miscarriage.

Causes

In most cases, it is not possible to explain why the miscarriage has occurred.

Most miscarriages are not caused by anything the mother has done.

Symptoms

Symptoms may include:

- bleeding from your vagina
- pain in your tummy

Sometimes there are no symptoms and the miscarriage is detected during an ultrasound scan.

How is a miscarriage confirmed?

A miscarriage will normally be diagnosed using an ultrasound scan. Sometimes you may need to have more than one scan.

You may also need to have blood tests.

What happens if a miscarriage is confirmed?

If the ultrasound scan confirms the miscarriage and that nothing remains in your womb, you may not need any further treatment.

If some of the pregnancy remains in your womb, your obstetrician and midwives will discuss the best treatment option for you.

Depending on your circumstances, your options may include:

Expectant management	This means waiting and letting 'nature take its course'.
Medical management	This means taking medication. This is done by inserting the medication into your vagina or giving you tablets to swallow.
Surgical management	This means having an operation to remove the pregnancy.

Recovering from a miscarriage

As your body recovers from the miscarriage, you may experience:

- bleeding from your vagina for 1 to 2 weeks
- crampy tummy pain

Your next period will usually be 4 to 6 weeks after a miscarriage.

When to get medical help

Some women have further complications during or after a miscarriage. Get help if you:

- have heavy bleeding from your vagina (especially if you feel dizzy or weak)
- have severe abdominal pain
- have smelly vaginal discharge
- feel unwell or feverish

Your emotions after a miscarriage

There is no right or wrong way to feel after a miscarriage.

Many women feel tearful and emotional. Others feel guilt, shock and anger.

Talk about how you feel

Try to be open about your feelings and to communicate with your partner, family or friends. Talk to your GP if you feel you are not coping.

Your partner may have different ways of coping. Try and spend time together.

When can I try for another baby?

Most doctors will advise you not to have sex until all of your miscarriage symptoms have gone. This is to reduce your risk of infection.

After this, you can try for another baby as soon as you and your partner feel physically and emotionally ready. This is different for everybody.

Week 14 to 26: The second trimester

Week 14

Your baby is covered in a fine hair called lanugo. They are starting to use their facial muscles to frown and squint.

Week 16

They are practicing breathing amniotic fluid in and out.

Week 18

Your baby's ears begin to stick out from their head, and they may even begin to hear. They will hear your heart beating and may hear other noises too.

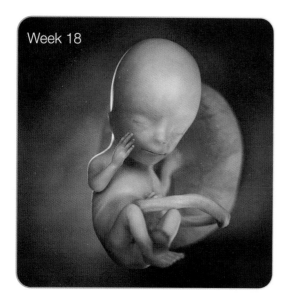

Week 18

Week 20

The halfway point! You may begin to feel your baby moving.

Week 22

Your baby's eyes have developed. Their skin looks wrinkled and will do until they gain more fatty tissue.

Week 24

Your baby is regularly sleeping and waking. Hair is growing on their head.

Week 26

Your baby is around 36 cm long, similar to the length of a scallion (spring onion).

They can:

- open their eyes
- hear your voice

Their heartbeat is stronger and can be heard by your healthcare team. Their inner ear has developed and they have a sense of balance.

Their teeth are developing. A white coating called 'vernix' may be developing on your baby's body.

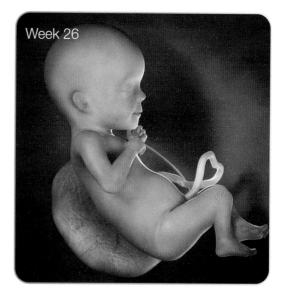

Week 26

Week 14 to 26: changes you may feel

Your baby's movements

This may feel like fluttering, bubbles popping or like the baby is poking you.

What to do

- Make a note of the first time you feel it.
- Be aware of your baby's movements. Contact your midwife, obstetrician or maternity hospital immediately if your baby's movements change, reduce or stop

Get to know your baby and encourage your partner to feel for movements.

Think about what your baby may be doing. Is your baby moving his or her arms and legs, or sucking a thumb?

More energy

You may feel more energy and less sickness than the first trimester.

What to do

- Enjoy this time and resist the urge to overdo it!

Back pain

This may be caused by your baby getting bigger.

Also, your ligaments stretch and soften to prepare you for the birth. This can cause pain.

What to do

- Wear flat or low-heeled shoes.
- Avoid standing for long periods of time and be aware of your posture.
- Avoid lifting heavy objects. Always bend your knees and keep your back straight when lifting.
- Do some back exercises (see page 41).
- A massage might help.
- Talk to your midwife, GP or obstetrician if the pain is severe. They might refer you to a chartered physiotherapist who could help.

Constipation

Hormonal changes can cause constipation.

What to do

- Eat foods that are high in fibre. For example, wholegrain breads, prunes and bran.
- Eat fresh fruit and vegetables daily.
- Exercise regularly.
- Drink plenty of water (1.5 to 2 litres per day).
- Only take iron supplements if you need them.

Correct toilet position if you are constipated

Heavy, swollen or restless legs and swollen ankles

This is caused by:

- the pressure of the growing baby
- extra fluid in your body
- slower blood circulation

What to do

- Do plenty of walking.
- Try not to cross your legs.
- Put your feet up when you can.
- Avoid long periods of standing.
- Use support stockings.
- Avoid tight clothing.
- Sleep on your left side, not on your back.
- If you get a leg cramp, pull your toes hard up towards your ankle or rub the muscle hard.
- Tell your GP, obstetrician or midwife at your next appointment.

Bleeding gums

For some pregnant women, hormonal changes can cause a build-up of plaque. This can cause the gums to bleed.

What to do

- Brush your teeth twice daily and floss once a day.
- See a dentist at least once during the pregnancy. Make sure to tell them that you are pregnant.

Emotional changes

During this trimester your tummy shape will show the first signs that you are going to become a mother.

As your baby starts moving, you may start to think more about yourself as a mother and the baby as a separate being.

You may:

- start imagining what your baby will be like
- think about yourself as a mother — and change your behaviours to reflect this
- feel emotional or sensitive about your body changing and getting bigger

What to do

Share your thoughts and feelings with your partner, support person, friends and family. This will help you to deal with any worries you may have.

If these feelings are very intense or severe, talk to your GP, midwife or obstetrician.

Sleep on your side

Your sleep pattern may change when you become pregnant.

You may:

- find it difficult to fall asleep
- sleep for longer than before
- have strange dreams about the baby or the birth – this is normal

Sleeping on your side is often more comfortable than sleeping on your back, especially after about 16 weeks.

Pillows

Try placing a pillow between your legs or supporting your bump with pillows.

Reducing the risk of stillbirth

As well as being more comfortable, researchers have found that sleeping on your side significantly reduces the risk of stillbirth.

Don't worry if you wake up on your back. Simply turn to your side before trying to return to sleep.

See your GP or obstetrician if you have:

- vaginal bleeding
- severe abdominal pain
- reduced movements
- a gush of fluid from your vagina

News of a possible abnormality

Being told that there is something wrong with your baby, or even that there may be something wrong, is extremely difficult.

You may get this news during an ultrasound or after other antenatal screening tests.

Decisions

Suddenly you are faced with decisions you never expected to make. These include whether you should have more invasive tests done, or even more painful decisions about the future of the pregnancy.

Emotions

You may feel alone, and over the coming days you may experience a range of different emotions. As you are dealing with anxiety, grief and sadness it can be very difficult to make decisions.

Ask questions

Make sure you understand exactly what you are being told. Do not be afraid to ask questions. Your obstetrician, midwives and GP are there to support you. It may help to bring someone with you to appointments, and to write down any questions you may have.

Your healthcare team should explain everything to you in a way that you can understand, but if they are using medical terms stop them and ask them to explain them. If English is not your primary language, ask for an interpreter.

Be informed

Try and gather as much information as you can from reliable sources. For some of the more common conditions, lots of information is available. For others, you may have to speak to specialised doctors like paediatricians or geneticists (specialists in inherited diseases).

Ask what supports are available. Your maternity hospital may be able to refer you to see a counsellor.

Deciding what to do

Only you, and your partner if you have one, can decide on the right decision for your family and for your baby. It may seem like no option is right for you. Trust in yourself: you will arrive at the right decision for you, and it is normal to change your mind often until this occurs.

If you choose to continue the pregnancy, you may have anxieties about the birth and what to expect when your baby is born. Talk to your healthcare team. They will give you information and support.

Depending on your situation, it may be a good idea to meet with the neonatologist (doctor who will be caring for your baby) so they can discuss the care your baby will need. Many maternity hospitals also have specialist midwives who offer extra support and provide you with information.

Sometimes the right decision for your family is to end the pregnancy. Your healthcare team will discuss this option with you. They will discuss the type of termination of pregnancy most suitable for your situation. They will also discuss your options in terms of where the procedure is performed. Think about whether you would like to see and hold your baby, and ask if this is an option.

There is no right or wrong way to feel when faced with such difficult choices. It is normal to grieve for your baby, and for the future that will now be different to the one you may have imagined. Try and talk to your partner or a trusted support person. You are not alone.

Week 27 to birth: The third trimester

Week 28

Your baby now has eyelashes and is gaining weight.

Week 30

Your baby's eyes are wide open quite a lot of the time. They may have hair.

Week 32

Your baby's toenails are visible! Their nervous system is continuing to develop. They are practising breathing. Right now your baby is about the size of a butternut squash.

Week 34

Your baby can now detect light. Their fingernails are growing.

Week 34

Week 36

Your baby is gaining about 227g (half a pound) a week.

Conditions are getting crowded but you should still feel definite movements from your baby.

Keep a note of your baby's movements

Contact the hospital if you cannot feel your baby moving or your baby is moving less than usual.

Week 38

Your baby now has a firm grasp. All the organs and features are now in place. You may be feeling excited to meet your baby.

Week 40: full-term

Only 5% of babies arrive on their due date! So don't be too disappointed if you have to wait a little longer.

Your baby may weigh 2.9 kg or more (6.5lb) – they come in all different shapes and sizes.

Congratulations, you have grown a human from one tiny cell!

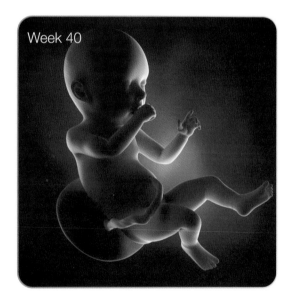

Week 40

Week 27 onwards: changes you may feel

Braxton Hicks or uterine contractions

During late pregnancy, your uterus may contract and relax. These are known as Braxton Hicks contractions.

Braxton Hicks are different to labour contractions because they:

- are not frequent
- are usually irregular
- don't last long, usually less than a minute and don't get more intense

What to do
- Walk around.
- Relax and take deep breaths.
- If they do not stop or if they become more intense, call your maternity unit or hospital, obstetrician or midwife.

Stretch marks

You may notice red stretch marks on your tummy and breasts. They may be itchy and feel tight.

Whether you get these or not depends on your genes and skin type.

It is doubtful whether creams and oils will help. However, they can be pleasant to use and make your skin feel less dry. Usually stretch marks will fade after the pregnancy.

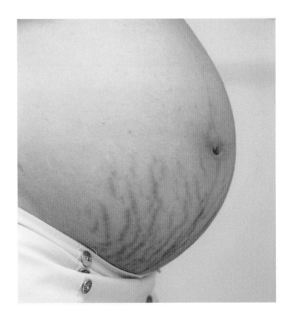

Heartburn

This is a burning feeling in your chest and throat. It is caused by the pressure a growing baby is putting on your stomach.

What to do
- Eat smaller meals.
- Avoid spicy or fried food.
- Avoid eating for the couple of hours before you go to bed.
- Sleep propped up with lots of pillows.
- Talk to your GP, obstetrician, pharmacist or midwife about medication.

Haemorrhoids (piles)

These are swellings in and around your anus. They may be itchy, painful or bleed.

What to do

- Eat foods high in fibre like oats, wholegrain bread and pasta, fruit and vegetables, potatoes with their skin on, peas, beans and legumes.
- Drink plenty of water.
- Avoid standing for long periods.
- Take gentle exercise.
- Your pharmacist, GP, midwife or obstetrician may recommend a cream.
- Avoid becoming constipated or straining on the toilet.

Straining

Your poo can become hard when you are not pooing as often as usual. This can mean you have to push quite hard to get the poo out. This is known as straining.

Straining puts pressure on the veins in your lower rectum (back passage) and causes piles. Straining can also damage piles and make them bleed. It can push internal piles to the outside.

Carpal tunnel syndrome (CTS)

Carpal tunnel syndrome (CTS) is caused by swelling in your hands that can cause a nerve to become squeezed.

Symptoms of this include:

- pins and needles
- pain or numbness in your middle fingers and hands

This is often worse at night.

What to do

- Put your hands in cold water.
- Raise your hands on a cushion in the evenings so they are higher than your heart.
- Squeeze a soft ball.
- Talk to your GP, midwife, obstetrician or physiotherapist.

Varicose veins

This is when veins in the legs or vulva become swollen. They usually return to normal after birth.

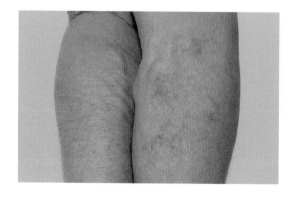

What to do

- Try not to sit with legs crossed.
- Sit with your feet up.
- Avoid standing for long periods.

- Try support stockings.
- Sleep with your legs higher than your body.

If your bump feels itchy

Mild itching of your bump is normal as your skin starts to stretch. Pregnancy hormones can also increase the blood-flow to the skin. This makes it feel hot and itchy.

What to do

- Wear loose clothing.
- Don't use strong detergents or very scented soaps and shower gels — these can irritate the skin.
- Moisturise your skin - try different ones to see what one works best for you.
- Contact your GP or obstetrician if the itch is severe or you notice a rash.

Anxiety

Anxiety is an unpleasant feeling of unease such as worry or fear. It can be mild, moderate or severe.

Symptoms can include:

- feeling restless, irritable and constantly on edge
- having difficulty concentrating
- dizziness
- excessive sweating
- palpitations (heartbeats that are more noticeable)
- difficulty in sleeping

It is very common to experience anxiety about giving birth and becoming a parent.

What to do

- Talk to your partner, support person, friends and family.
- Stick to a well-balanced diet and take exercise. This can help mild symptoms.
- See if mindfulness and guided meditation, including apps and videos, can help.
- If you have symptoms of anxiety which are becoming worse or if you have a history of an anxiety disorder, speak to your GP, midwife or obstetrician about it.

Other emotional changes

You are just a few weeks away from meeting your baby. Many pregnant women can hardly wait, while others may find it daunting.

Changes

Thoughts and feelings about the responsibility of becoming a mother often continue. You may have worries about becoming a parent and the changes this will bring. You may be feeling fed up of being pregnant.

It can be an exciting time as you prepare for your baby's arrival. You may be preparing for maternity leave or you may be 'nesting' – getting your home ready for a new baby.

Due date

As your due date approaches it is normal to feel more anxious about the birth. Have faith in your body, it knows exactly what to do.

Sleep

Your sleep will get disrupted towards the end of the third trimester. This is normal and can have an impact on your mental health. Rest when you can.

Talk

It is important to make time to talk to your support person or partner to share your feelings, hopes and fears.

When to get urgent medical help

Emergencies during pregnancy

There are some warnings signs to watch out for during pregnancy. They could mean you're experiencing pregnancy complications or a medical emergency. Some are signs of miscarriage.

Here are some severe pregnancy symptoms to watch out for:

Bleeding from your vagina

Contact your GP, midwife or obstetrician immediately if you are bleeding from your vagina.

Severe or sharp pains in your tummy

Contact your midwife or GP immediately if:

- the pain is severe
- the pain feels like tightening (this could be a sign you are having a contraction)
- you have any bleeding from your vagina
- the pain is in your upper tummy area, especially on the right-hand side (this could be a sign of pre-eclampsia)
- you have symptoms like pain when you pass urine or when you need to wee, high temperature, a need to pee more than normal and cloudy or smelly wee (these are signs of a urinary tract infection)

Headaches during pregnancy

Contact your midwife or GP immediately if you have a severe headache or a headache with any of the following symptoms:

- pronounced swelling of your hands, feet, ankles, neck or face, particularly if sudden
- flashing lights in your eyes or blurred vision
- you have recently been diagnosed with high blood pressure

These are all signs of pre-eclampsia (page 90).

Distress and thoughts of self-harm

Mental health problems in pregnancy are common and can be treated.

Contact your midwife, GP or your nearest hospital emergency department (A&E) immediately if you feel:

- distressed
- extremely low
- severe anxiety
- in crisis
- at risk of hurting or harming yourself

Breathlessness or chest pain

See your GP, obstetrician, midwife or hospital emergency department immediately if:

- the breathlessness is sudden or severe
- you have breathlessness and chest pain, heart palpitations or dizziness

Leg pain and swollen calf

Contact your GP or hospital emergency department immediately if your calf is red, swollen and hot.

Your baby's movements

You will probably become aware of your baby's movements between 16 and 24 weeks of pregnancy.

You may feel a fluttering in your tummy, or a rolling sensation that feels like wind moving in your tummy.

Most babies settle into a pattern by 24 weeks.

If your baby stops moving or moves less often

Your baby's movements are important because:

- Feeling your baby move is a sign that they are well.
- When your baby's movements reduce or stop, sometimes this can be the first sign that your baby is unwell.

Talk to your GP or midwife if:

- you do not feel your baby moving
- you are feeling less movement than usual

Even if this happens many times, get checked each time.

Home dopplers and apps

Do not use a home doppler or an app. They should never replace getting checked by your GP, obstetrician or midwife.

How often should my baby move?

There is no set number of movements that is normal. Every baby is different.

You need to become aware of what is normal for your baby. From 16 to 24 weeks on, you should feel your baby move more and more up until 32 weeks. From week 32 onwards the movements stay roughly the same until you give birth.

Reasons you may not feel your baby moving:

- You are very busy or active.
- Your placenta (afterbirth) is at the front of your uterus (womb).
- If you drink alcohol or smoke.
- If you are taking certain medications.

It is not true that babies move less towards the end of pregnancy.

You should continue to feel your baby moving throughout the pregnancy.

Talk to your midwife, obstetrician or maternity hospital immediately if you are worried about your baby's movements. Do not wait until tomorrow.

Premature labour

Premature labour is labour that starts too early (before 37 weeks). It can cause your baby to be born too soon.

Babies who are born too early are at risk of health problems. They often need special care in the hospital.

One in 16 women will give birth prematurely. Over 4,500 babies are born preterm in Ireland every year.

Signs of premature labour

Fluid, discharge or bleeding

- a gush of fluid from your vagina or water leaking from your vagina
- a sudden increase in the amount of discharge from your vagina, or sudden change in the type of vaginal discharge
- bleeding from your vagina

Aches or pains

- cramps like period pains
- low dull back-ache that feels different than usual
- pain in your tummy
- sudden feeling of increased pressure or the feeling that the baby is pushing down
- contractions – tightenings of your womb that come often and do not go away
- contractions that get stronger and are coming closer together
- the feeling that something "is not right"

If you have any of these signs, contact your maternity unit or midwife immediately.

How can I help my baby to be born at the right time?

- Try to stop smoking and ask others not to smoke around you.
- Prepare and store food safely (see page 35).
- Avoid the foods that are not recommended during pregnancy (see page 36).
- If you have had a late miscarriage in the past or treatments on your cervix, talk to your obstetrician. Sometimes a stitch can be placed around your cervix to stop it from opening too early.
- Take time to rest every day.
- See your GP or obstetrician if you have smelly vaginal discharge or pain or burning when you pee.

More information and support:

Irish Premature Babies support group: irishprematurebabies.com

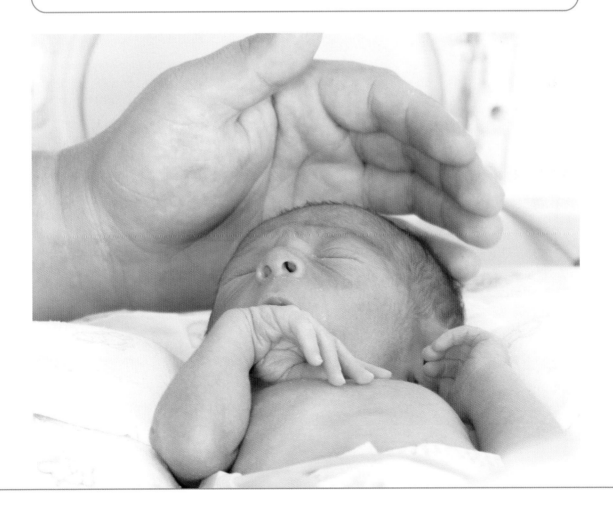

Pregnancies that need more care

Conditions

High blood pressure and pre-eclampsia

Your GP, midwife or obstetrician will check your blood pressure each time you visit them during pregnancy. If your blood pressure is high, your heart has to work harder to pump blood around the body. High blood pressure or hypertension affects between 10% to 15% of pregnancies.

A rise in blood pressure can be the first sign of a condition called pre-eclampsia. Most cases of pre-eclampsia are mild. More serious cases can cause complications for mothers and for babies.

As well as causing high blood pressure, pre-eclampsia can cause:

- swelling of the hands, feet or face
- protein in the urine

Pre-eclampsia can affect your baby's growth. Sometimes you may need to take medication.

Pre-eclampsia can sometimes mean that your baby will need to be born early.

Protein in urine

Having some protein in your urine can be normal during pregnancy. However, high levels of protein could be a sign of pre-eclampsia.

Tips for reducing blood pressure

- eat healthily
- reduce the salt in your diet
- keep active with exercise such as swimming or walking

Gestational diabetes

Gestational diabetes is a type of diabetes that occurs in pregnant women. It means that the insulin in your body is not working properly. Your body cannot get sugar from your blood into your cells. This can cause problems for mothers and for babies.

The good news is that eating healthily and staying active will help you to prevent gestational diabetes, and, even if you do develop it, it can be treated. Usually gestational diabetes will disappear after your baby is born.

A specialised blood test called an oral glucose tolerance test can detect gestational diabetes.

How gestational diabetes is treated

Your blood sugars will be monitored. You may be referred to a clinical nurse or midwife specialist in diabetes. They will teach you how to monitor your blood sugars at home.

Healthy eating and staying active during the pregnancy will help.

Between 10 to 20% of women with gestational diabetes will need insulin injections.

Placenta praevia

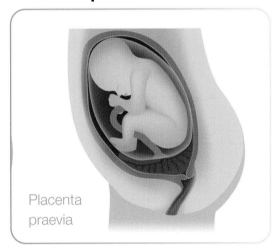

Placenta praevia

During pregnancy, the placenta (also called the afterbirth) provides your baby with all the nutrients and oxygen they need.

Placenta praevia means that your placenta is lying unusually low in your uterus (womb), near to or covering your cervix.

This may increase your risk of bleeding during the pregnancy or at the time of birth. You may be advised to rest at home or to come into hospital at the end of your pregnancy.

If the placenta is covering the cervix or is very near the cervix, it may block your baby's exit. If this happens, you may need a caesarean section.

Babies who are small or growing slowly

You may be told that your baby is "small for gestational age". This means they are smaller than expected at a particular stage of pregnancy.

This might be noticed during a physical examination or an ultrasound scan. If your baby is small, your pregnancy will be monitored more closely.

Smoking during pregnancy and some medical conditions can cause your baby to be small.

Your obstetrician may suggest birthing the baby if there are signs that your baby is in distress or becoming tired.

Breech presentation

By 36 weeks, your baby's head should be facing downwards in the womb. If your baby is breech, this means their bottom is downwards, or their feet are downwards instead. This can make the birth more challenging.

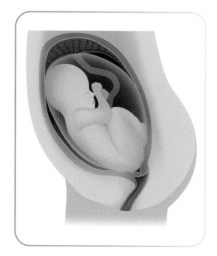

External cephalic version (ECV)

You may be offered an external cephalic version (ECV) if your baby is breech. This is a procedure carried out by a specially-trained obstetrician. Gentle pressure is applied to your abdomen (stomach). This helps the baby turn from a breech to a head-down position.

If ECV does not work, you will usually be offered a caesarean birth. See page 128.

Did you know?

If your baby is still breech after 36 weeks, they will need an ultrasound scan of their hips after birth. Ask your paediatrician or GP about this.

Expecting twins or more?

Expecting twins, triplets or even quadruplets? A 'multiple pregnancy' is the term used when you are pregnant with two or more babies. Almost 2% of births in Ireland are twin births. A woman is more likely to have twins if there are twins in her family. Advances in fertility treatments have led to twins, triplets and even quadruplets becoming more common. Most ultrasounds should detect multiple births by 14 weeks.

Type of multiple pregnancy	How this happens
Identical twins (33% of twin births)	One fertilised egg splits in two. Each baby has the exact same DNA, so they will look very alike and be the same gender.
Non-identical twins (66% of twin births)	Two eggs are fertilised by two sperm at the same time. Babies may be different genders and will be no more alike than any other brothers and sisters.
Triplets	Triplets can be non-identical, two may be identical with one non-identical, or all three may be identical.

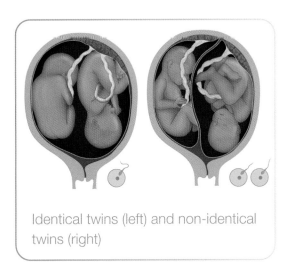

Identical twins (left) and non-identical twins (right)

Why is carrying two or more babies different?

Most women with twins or multiple pregnancies will have a healthy pregnancy and healthy babies but complications are more common.

Problems more common

Any problems that arise in pregnancy, such as pre-eclampsia and anaemia, are more common with twins.

The most common risk is of premature labour which could mean that your babies are born prematurely.

Close monitoring

If your babies share a placenta, they will be monitored very closely to ensure both babies are growing well.

The birth

You will be advised to have the birth in a hospital and have consultant-led (obstetrician) care. You may also be advised to have your babies in a hospital that has a neonatal unit.

Your labour will be monitored closely and there will be more healthcare professionals than usual present.

There is a higher chance that you may be advised to have a caesarean birth
(see page 128).

How to cope with two babies at once?

- Consider going on maternity leave early.
- When your babies are born, it will be busy – take any help and support available.
- Establishing a routine early may also help.

It is possible to breastfeed twins and even triplets.

Support for families of 'multiples' at imba.ie

Thinking about breastfeeding

Benefits of breastfeeding

Now is a good time to start thinking about how you would like to feed your baby. More and more mothers in Ireland are breastfeeding their babies.

Breast milk is important for your baby

Your milk is unique and is made especially for your baby to meet your baby's growing needs.

Breast milk is convenient. It is always:

- fresh
- available
- the correct temperature

It helps protect your baby from infections such as chest, ear and tummy infections and from other illnesses.

Breastfeeding reduces your baby's risk of:

- constipation
- an upset tummy
- obesity

Breastfeeding is important for mothers too

Breastfeeding helps you bond with your baby. It also helps your uterus (womb) return to normal size more quickly.

It reduces your risk of:

- breast cancer
- ovarian cancer
- diabetes

Breastfeeding burns calories, and may help you regain your pre-pregnancy weight.

> **Convenient**
>
> Breastfeeding saves you time and money. You don't need to prepare bottles and formula or carry them with you when out and about.

Preparing to breastfeed

There is no physical preparation that you need to do to breastfeed. You will notice some changes in your breasts during pregnancy. This is your body getting ready for feeding your baby.

You may be planning to breastfeed your baby and wondering how it's done.

It can help to prepare for breastfeeding to read some of the practical tips in this section and from page 138.

These tips can help you to know what to expect when feeding your new baby.

You can get advice and get answers to your questions from:

- your midwife
- your public health nurse
- your GP
- lactation consultants on mychild.ie
- your local breastfeeding support group (see page 149) – pregnant women are welcome

> Breastfeeding is the most natural way to feed your baby. It is a skill that you and your baby develop over the first days and weeks. With the right support, most mothers can start breastfeeding and continue for as long as they want to.

Changes to your breasts during pregnancy

You may have noticed your breasts changing as your pregnancy progresses.

Early on

Early on in the pregnancy you may notice a tingling or tender sensation in your breasts.

As your pregnancy progresses:

- the nipples and the areola (the area around the nipples) may darken in colour
- the veins on the surface of your breasts may become more noticeable

Liquid gold

From about 16 weeks, your breasts are ready to start producing milk. This is the first milk or colostrum. It is yellow in colour and is often called liquid gold.

Blood

Sometimes blood may leak from your nipples. Always get your breasts checked by a GP if you notice blood-stained nipple discharge.

Last few weeks

In the last few weeks of pregnancy, your nipples and breasts become larger.

Lumps

Breast lumps can sometimes occur during pregnancy. Most of the time, these are benign and caused by hormonal changes.

Always get checked by your GP if you get new breast lumps or an existing lump changes during pregnancy.

Preparing your body

Eating healthy food will help your body produce breast milk. Apart from this, you don't need to do anything differently to help prepare for breastfeeding. Nature takes care of all that!

A note about bras

As your breasts grow, your bra needs to fit you well.

Make sure:

- your bra is not too tight or loose
- the strap at the back doesn't cut in
- your breasts fill the fabric of the cup with no loose fabric
- there is no bulging over the top, at the sides or underneath the bra
- the shoulder straps stay in place without digging in
- the strap around the back and the front underband lie close to your body and are roughly at the same level

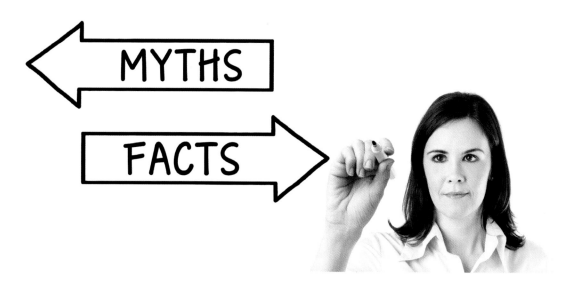

Breastfeeding myth-busters

When you're pregnant, you may notice that everyone around you has an opinion, or has advice for you. This can continue right through your child's early years. It is a good idea to get used to it, and to develop some strategies to deal with it!

Parenting choices

Family and friends usually mean well, and genuinely want to help you. Try to remember that their parenting choices are not necessarily the right ones for you or for your baby.

If you were born in Ireland, there is a good chance that your mother may have chosen to formula feed you. At the time, formula companies were allowed to market their products without the same restrictions as today. Mothers genuinely believed they were giving their babies the best start. However, years have passed since then.

Research

The research is stronger than ever about the importance of breastfeeding. Here are some common myths you may hear when talking about breastfeeding:

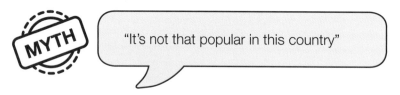

Over 55% of women in Ireland choose to breastfeed their babies. Yes, this number is lower than other European countries but still represents over half.

Almost all women are able to produce enough breast milk. The size and shape of your breasts or nipples doesn't matter. Early and frequent feeding is the best way to establish your supply.

Establishing your supply means that your supply of breast milk matches exactly what your baby needs. Breastfeeding is a supply and demand system. The more you breastfeed, the more milk your body produces.

 "Your partner will feel left out if you breastfeed"

There are still lots of ways partners can bond with the baby and plenty of ways they can help you.

For example:

- holding and cuddling the baby
- changing nappies
- burping the baby
- bathing the baby
- bringing the baby to you to be fed

They can also bring you water or snacks while you are feeding.

You can still have a sex life while breastfeeding.

 "Modern formula is just as good as breast milk"

No formula protects your baby from infections and diseases the way breast milk does. Formula is not sterile and needs to be safely prepared. If you decide to formula feed, your nurse or midwife will help you.

 "Breastfeeding hurts"

Breastfeeding shouldn't hurt. If it does, it usually means the baby is not positioned or attached (latched on) correctly. Your midwife, neonatal nurse, public health nurse, GP practice nurse or lactation consultant can help with this. See page 139 for tips on positioning and attachment.

"Breastfeeding will make your breasts sag"

Breastfeeding will not make your breasts sag. Sagging breasts are caused by pregnancy and by getting older. Pregnancy hormones can stretch the ligaments that support your breasts. The ageing process can also make breasts appear to sag. Wearing a well-fitting bra during pregnancy and while breastfeeding can help to combat this.

Questions about feeding your baby?

Ask your midwife, neonatal nurse, public health nurse, GP practice nurse or GP any questions you may have about feeding your baby. You can also live chat with a lactation consultant for free on mychild.ie

They may talk to you about:

Your baby's first few hours

Safe skin-to-skin contact with your baby early after birth will help get the first feed off to a good start. Holding your baby with their skin next to your skin will calm and relax you and your baby.

Breastfeeding in the first hour after birth provides food, comfort and a good start for your baby's immune system.

Rooming-in

Rooming-in means having your baby's cot beside your bed after the birth. Doing this for the first 24 hours after birth helps you to start breastfeeding and to bond.

Knowing when your baby needs to feed

Responsive feeding means you will know when your baby is getting hungry. This is feeding when your baby shows early feeding cues (signs) (see page 139).

Positioning and attachment

Positioning and attachment is sometimes called 'latching on'. The correct positioning and attachment of your baby to the breast will make breastfeeding much easier. There are lots of positions you can try.

Soothers

Avoid using soothers, especially in the early weeks of breastfeeding. These may decrease the number of feeds your baby wants. This in turn can interfere with how much breast milk your body produces.

Formula top-ups

Avoid giving your baby top-ups of formula milk if you are breastfeeding, unless you are told to do so for medical reasons.

Local support groups

Your local breastfeeding support group is a great way to get more information and advice and meet other parents at the same stage as you. See page 149.

Birthing your baby

Positive preparation for birth

As your due date beckons, you may begin to feel excited, expectant or even a little anxious. You may be fed up of being pregnant and eager to meet your baby.

Things that can help include:

Talk about it

Talk to:

- other mothers about their labours and births
- your doctors and midwives about the type of experience you might have

Visit the hospital

If you are giving birth in a hospital, you might find it helpful to go on a tour of the birthing suite. There may be a video of this you can watch.

Birth partner

Think about who you would like as your birth partner. Talk to your birth partner about things they can do to support you.

Childcare

Think about childcare arrangements for your other children.

Prepare your home

Make a list of the things you may need for your baby. Things that you need can be bought gradually over time. Friends and family may be able to lend you things. See page 177.

Prepare a safe place for your baby to sleep. For at least the first six months, this should be in the same room as you. See page 182.

You may find it helpful to cook meals that can be reheated after the baby is born.

Get ready to finish work

Try and get things organised at work a few weeks before your maternity leave starts, just in case you go into labour before your due date. You may not have as much time as you think you have!

Ask for help

Ask family and friends for help, especially during those first few weeks with a newborn.

Be healthy

Continue exercising and eating healthily.

Get rest

Rest when you can.

Enjoy this time

Do things that you enjoy and that you may not have as much time for when baby comes. This might include seeing friends or going to the hairdressers.

Things to remember

- Your body knows exactly what to do.
- Contractions are strong but their peak is short and they will pass.
- There are many people to help you along the way.

Trust yourself

Trust in yourself – you are strong, you've got this.

Know what to expect

Educate yourself – we all fear the unknown. Once you know what to expect, your anxiety may reduce. Mentally rehearse what labour might be like for you.

Be aware that sometimes complications can happen. Don't dwell on them, but be aware of them. Think about the need for a 'plan b' for a safe birth.

Some people find it helpful to write down their fears.

Positive thinking

Our minds are powerful painkillers. Practice positive thinking. Some women find visualisation techniques help during labour. For example, picture a flower opening with every contraction.

Pregnancy yoga, pregnancy pilates or hypnobirthing classes can be a great way to learn breathing and relaxation techniques.

Support from others

Surround yourself with support. Find people you can trust to talk to.

Get help if anxiety is:

- your main emotion
- affecting your life
- taking your joy

Talk to your GP, obstetrician or your midwife.

Mental and emotional preparation to give birth

Think about becoming a parent, whether for the first time or to another child:

- How would you like your baby to see you?
- What kind of parent would you like to be?
- Are there any challenges? Can you think of solutions?
- Write a letter to your unborn baby.

Preparing your body for birth

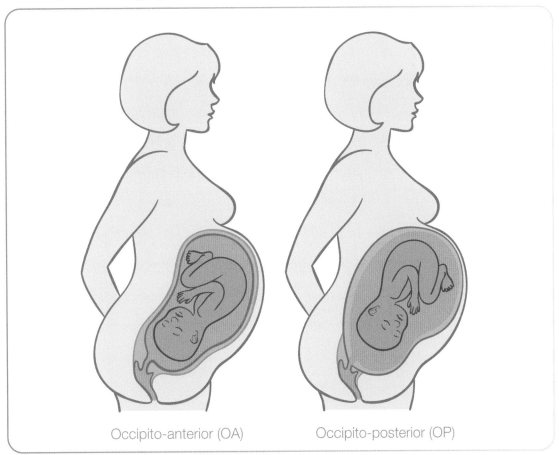

Occipito-anterior (OA)   Occipito-posterior (OP)

The best position for your baby to be in at the start of labour is with their head down and their back faced outwards towards your tummy. This is called the occipito-anterior (OA) position.

Helping your baby get into the best position

Sometimes babies may be head-down, but their back is facing your back. This is called the occipito-posterior (OP) position. The OP position may lead to a longer labour time.

'Optimal foetal positioning' is a theory developed by a midwife called Jean Sutton. This is about the movements and positions of a mother during the final weeks of pregnancy. She found that this could influence the baby's position in the womb.

Since then, many midwives and mothers are convinced that optimal foetal positioning techniques work. There is anecdotal evidence (individual stories) and testimonials, but not many clinical trials have been done. However, the techniques recommended are non-invasive and safe, and might be worth a try!

Optimal foetal positioning techniques

You can try these from 34 weeks onwards.

- Spend a lot of time kneeling upright, sitting upright or on your hands and knees.
- When you sit on a chair, make sure your knees are lower than your pelvis.
- Watch TV while kneeling on the floor.
- Sit on a dining chair. Lean on the back of the chair.
- Keep a wedge cushion in the car to tilt your pelvis forward.
- Don't cross your legs.
- Don't put your feet up.
- Sleep on your side.
- Swimming with your belly downwards may help - don't do the 'backstroke'.

Perineal massage

The perineum is the area of tissue between your vagina and your anus (back passage). Sometimes this area can be damaged during birth. Massaging your perineum from 34 weeks on may reduce this risk.

A good time to try perineal massage is after a bath or a shower which makes the perineum softer. You could also use an organic oil such as grape seed oil to make the massage more comfortable. Do not use scented or synthetic oils.

1. Get comfortable. A mirror may help.
2. Place a thumb just within the back wall of your vagina, resting your forefinger on your buttocks.
3. Press down a little towards your rectum (back passage).
4. Gently massage by moving your thumb and forefinger together in a U-shaped movement. Your aim is to massage the area inside your vagina.
5. This should be comfortable – you should feel a stretching sensation.
6. Aim for 5 minutes most days.
7. Tell your midwife or physiotherapist if you had a significant perineal tear in a previous pregnancy.

Do not do perineal massage if you have:
- genital herpes
- thrush
- bacterial vaginosis
- any vaginal infections

Preparing your other children

During the pregnancy

"It might help me if you read me stories about baby brothers and sisters."

"Maybe bring me with you when you are visiting friends who have babies."

"Bring me to the GP for some of your appointments later in the pregnancy. I might hear the baby's heartbeat!"

"Chat to me about the pregnancy. Let me help you get ready! I'd love to pick out an outfit for the baby."

After the birth

"Please know that I will have lots of feelings. Sometimes I might even be angry or sad but that's ok. It doesn't mean I don't love my new baby brother or sister."

"Try and have some special time just for me, even 10 minutes is enough."

"I love helping, let me help when the baby comes! I could fetch nappies for the baby or do other tasks depending on my age."

"Talk to me when you are feeding the baby or changing their nappy."

"The love you give me teaches me how to love others."

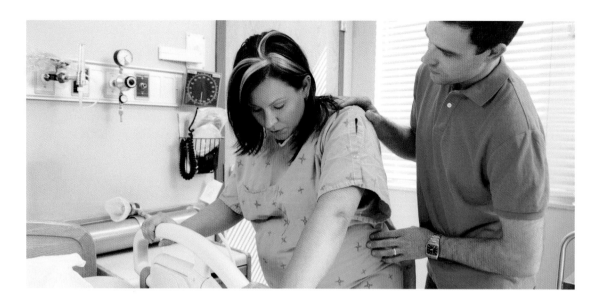

How your birth partner can help

Your midwife will be with you during your labour and birth. You can also have another person stay with you throughout. They can be your own personal source of support. This person can be your partner, your mother, your sister, your friend, but ideally someone you know and trust.

> Research shows that women who have good support in labour:
>
> - use less pain-relieving drugs
> - have a more satisfying childbirth experience
> - have a better chance of a natural vaginal birth

A note for birth partners – how you can help

Just be there! You are sharing this special journey. You are an important part. You are not in the way.

Your support can help your loved one even in the early stages of labour before you go to the hospital.

Birth wishes

Talk to her during early pregnancy about her wishes. During labour, you may need to talk about these wishes for her if she is busy focusing on breathing.

Discuss techniques to deal with contractions. Practice them. During labour, respect her wishes. She will know at the time what she needs the most.

Plan ahead

Before the labour, have a plan in place for how you will get to the birth. For example, keep some change handy to pay for hospital parking.

Bring snacks for yourself and perhaps a change of t-shirt.

When labour starts

Make sure she is well supported and relaxed. Help her by practising any relaxation techniques you have learned.

Try not to talk or ask questions during a contraction. She may need to focus and talking could distract her. Maintaining eye contact can help as it may focus attention away from the pain.

Massage can help during labour. However, some women become very sensitive and find any touch annoying.

The birth

Remind her about different birthing positions. You may need to support her in some of these positions.

Ask questions, support her wishes, be aware that plans may need to change depending on how events unfold. Together, as a team, share decisions.

When the baby is born

Think about whether you would like to cut the umbilical cord.

Sometimes newborn babies look very different to babies who are a few weeks old. If you are not prepared for this, it can come as a surprise.

Be prepared for them to be wrinkled. They may have skin redness or dryness or a white coating (called vernix) on the skin. The baby's head may be an unusual shape after passing through the birth canal. This is all normal.

Your birth wishes and preferences

Writing a list of your birth wishes may help you to think about the choices you may have and explore the options. This is sometimes called a 'birth plan'.

Your birth wishes will depend on:

- what you want
- your medical history
- your own circumstances
- the maternity options available locally

You should always talk about your wishes with your midwife or obstetrician. What may be safe and practical for one pregnant woman, may not be a good idea for another. Discuss your wishes early.

> Keep an open mind when writing your birth wishes - sometimes plans may need to change.

Things to include in your birth wishes:

Where to give birth

Your GP or midwife will discuss your choices.

Birth partner

Think about who will be your birth partner. Do you want them in the room when your baby is being born? If you had to have a caesarean birth, would you like them there?

Birthing equipment

List any equipment you want to use, such as TENS machines, yoga balls or birthing mats. You may have to bring your own equipment. Check with your midwife. Maternity hospitals may have guidelines on their use.

Monitoring during labour

Every baby is monitored during labour to make they are not in distress. There are different ways of doing this. Write down if you want to discuss how you would like to be monitored during labour.

Keeping active during labour and birth positions

Keep active for as long as you feel comfortable. Make it clear in your birth wishes if you want to move around during labour. Try out various positions, such as sitting, standing, kneeling, squatting. List the ones you might like to try during labour.

Dealing with contractions

There are many options to help with contractions. Some women try a combination of methods. You might like to list your preferred methods.

Bear in mind that you may need more, or less, medication than you had planned.

Episiotomy

An episiotomy is a cut in the perineum (the area between the vagina and anus). This may be needed if the baby needs to be born quickly.

Write down if this is something you would like to discuss with your obstetrician or midwife.

Skin-to-skin contact

Your baby is dried immediately after the birth and placed onto your chest. A towel is then placed over your baby's back to keep them warm. This is called skin-to-skin contact.

Your midwife will be there to help you. This is so important for mother and baby that it is on everyone's list.

Birth of the placenta (afterbirth)

Talk to your midwife about the birth of your placenta and any special requirements you may have.

Vitamin K for your baby

Vitamin K is needed to make the blood clot properly. All babies are given vitamin K with your consent. You might like to state whether you consent to this.

Breastfeeding

If you are planning to breastfeed your baby, it is very important to include this. Many newborn babies breastfeed soon after birth.

Packing for the hospital

Below is a list of suggested items to pack if you're giving birth in a hospital.

Hospitals have limited space for personal items, so try to pack lightly. It is best to leave valuables at home.

What to pack for you

Files and medication

- pregnancy records, including birth wishes or plan
- any prescribed medication

Clothes for hospital stay

- 2 comfortable maternity bras, nursing bras or support vests
- dressing gown
- 3 to 4 nightgowns or pyjamas (light ones – hospitals can be warm)
- a front-opening nightshirt or pyjamas if you want to breastfeed
- an old t-shirt or shirt for labour
- underwear – choose large cotton or disposable
- a pair of socks for labour (your feet can get cold)

Footwear

- slippers
- flip-flops or other waterproof sandals for shower

Hair clips and bands

- hair clips and hair bands to keep your hair off your face during labour

Towels and toiletries

- towel (choose dark colours to avoid staining) for each day you're in hospital
- toiletries: lip balm, toothbrush, hairbrush, face cloth, tissues
- breast pads and nipple cream
- 2 large packs of maternity sanitary towels
- small bottle of hand sanitiser

Snacks and water bottle

- healthy snacks (such as fruit and rice cakes)
- refillable water bottle

Birthing equipment

- any birthing equipment like a birthing ball or TENS machine if you plan on using one

Other items

- phone and phone charger
- camera
- things to help you pass the time and relax (books, magazines, newspapers or music and earphones)

You might also consider bringing your own pillow to hospital. If you do, use a coloured pillowcase so it is not mistaken for a hospital pillow.

After the birth

- pen and paper (you may have to record baby's feeds)
- change for the car park
- loose-fitting clothes for the trip home (which fit you at 26 weeks pregnant)

What to pack for your baby

Clothes
All baby clothes should be washed before packing.

- 6 baby vests, 6 babygros and 6 bibs
- cardigan
- hat

Towels and blankets

- pre-washed baby towels
- 2 cellular baby blankets

Sheets and cloths

- 2 cot sheets (if your hospital doesn't provide them)
- muslin cloths

Nappies

- 24 newborn nappies
- 1 roll of cotton wool or pack of cotton wool balls
- baby wipes
- nappy cream

Car seat

- car seat (to be brought in on the day you are going home)

Your birth partner

Tell your birth partner to have their own small bag ready too. They will need a change of clothes, toiletries, change for the car park and a phone charger. You'll have enough to think about!

Things to do

- Plan your route to the hospital – do you know the parking arrangements?
- Arrange childcare for your other children.
- Have the number for the maternity ward or admissions office – save it on your phone and stick it up at home.
- Learn your Eircode – this will help an ambulance find your home quickly if you need one.

Recognising labour

The word labour means 'work'. Labour is the work your uterus (womb) does to help the baby come out.

This involves the uterus tightening ('contracting') and resting. It then tightens or contracts again.

This helps the neck of your womb, known as the cervix, get thinner ('efface') and open ('dilate').

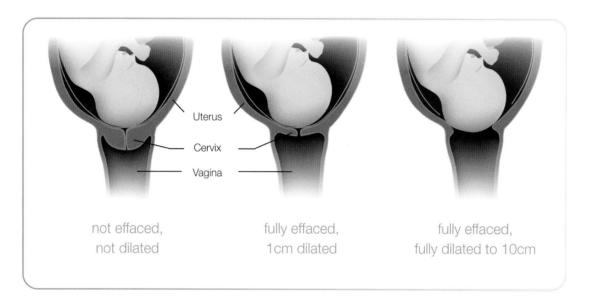

Uterus		
Cervix		
Vagina		

not effaced, not dilated   fully effaced, 1cm dilated   fully effaced, fully dilated to 10cm

How long does labour last?

Every labour and birth is different, and labour can be unpredictable. Be prepared to be flexible with your plans. It is hard to know how long your labour will last. Most first babies arrive after 12 to 20 hours.

The signs of labour

Most women go into labour within 7 to 10 days of their due date. If you are not sure whether you are in labour or not, call your midwife or maternity unit.

There is no one definite sign that tells you when labour is starting. The following are examples of what you can expect:

Regular contractions

During a contraction, your uterus (womb) tightens and rests.

When these contractions last for more than 30 seconds, and begin to feel stronger, labour may have started.

These contractions become more frequent, stronger and longer as labour progresses.

Some women get mild or less strong contractions throughout pregnancy. These are called Braxton Hicks contractions (page 81).

Back ache

This is aching heavy feeling in the lower back. It is similar to what some women experience during a period.

A 'show'

During pregnancy, a plug of mucus forms at the cervix (the neck of the womb). This helps to seal the womb during pregnancy.

In early labour, this may come out of the vagina. This small amount of sticky pink mucus is called the 'show'.

It may be mixed with a small amount of blood. If a large amount of blood is present, go straight to your maternity unit or hospital.

Your waters breaking or releasing

In the uterus (or womb), your baby is inside a bag of fluid. This is known as the amniotic sac.

When the baby is ready to be born, it is normal for the bag of water to release. Sometimes this can happen before labour begins.

You may notice fluid leaking from your vagina or a gush of fluid. Call your maternity unit or hospital when this happens. Do not use tampons.

Other signs

- nausea
- vomiting
- diarrhoea
- "nesting"
- excitement
- nervousness

When to go to the hospital or call your home birth midwife

There is a particular point in labour when you will need to:

- go to your maternity unit or hospital
- call your midwife if having a home birth

This is when your contractions are 5 minutes apart and are getting stronger or your waters break.

You may be asked to go to hospital or contact your home birth midwife earlier if you live a long distance away.

You will also have to go to hospital (regardless of home birth plans) if:

- you are bleeding from your vagina
- your baby is not moving as much as usual

How to time your contractions

Timing your contractions may help you decide if you are in true labour or not. Start timing your contractions when you feel they are getting stronger or closer together.

Time three contractions in a row. Use a mobile phone app or a watch which has a second hand for minutes.

Write down:

- the start time of each contraction
- the end time of each contraction
- the time when the next contraction starts
- how strong they feel

This will help you to know:

- how long each contraction lasts
- how far apart the contractions are

Ways to deal with early labour at home

- Use the focussed breathing you learned at antenatal classes.
- Have a bath.
- Go for a short walk.
- Try to find something light to watch, read or listen to during contractions.
- Go to the toilet to pass urine (wee) regularly.
- Eat small amounts of food. Drink water. Chew ice cubes.
- Ask your birth partner to give you a massage.
- Use your TENS machine if you have one.

Think positive thoughts, you'll be meeting your baby soon. Picture tiny fingers and toes. What will your baby look like?

Let them know and bring your file

Phone your midwife or maternity unit before going to the hospital. Bring your antenatal card or your pregnancy notes and your bag. (Some hospitals now have electronic records).

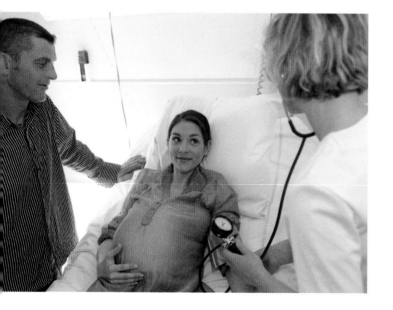

What happens next

When you get to the hospital

A midwife will assess you. They will talk to you about what signs you may have.

They may offer to do a vaginal (internal) examination to see how your labour is progressing.

Early labour

If you are still in early labour and live nearby, you may prefer to go home. You will then go to the hospital when labour gets stronger.

Admitted to hospital

If you need to stay in hospital, you will be admitted to the antenatal ward or to the birthing suite.

Your partner may be asked to go home for a few hours if this happens during the middle of the night. This is because other mothers and babies in the ward may be sleeping.

Your partner will be able to stay with you if you are:

- in strong active labour
- admitted directly to a single birthing suite room

The phases of labour

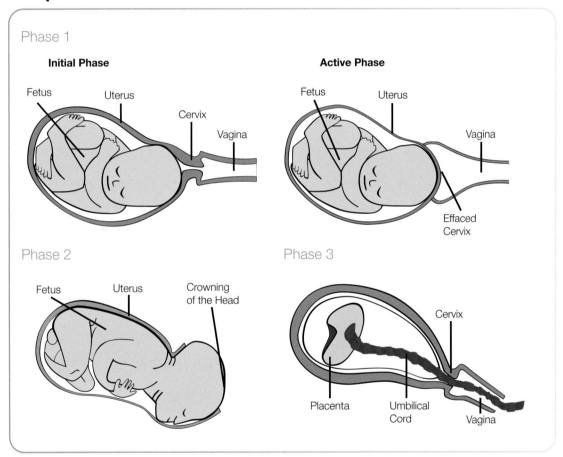

Phase 1 of labour is...

Labour! Your contractions become stronger, more frequent and the neck of your womb (your cervix) becomes thin and dilates to 10cm.

Phase 2 of labour is...

The birth of your baby. You will have more strong contractions. You will feel the urge to push. You will be asked to push when you have a contraction. Your baby will be born.

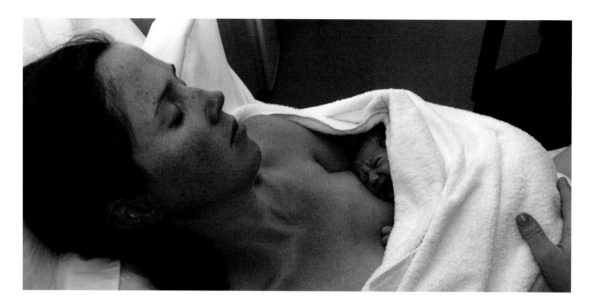

Phase 3 of labour is...

Birthing the placenta (afterbirth). During this stage you will be pushing the placenta out.

Becoming a parent and recovery

You will be resting and spending time with your baby. This is a good time to begin breastfeeding. See page 138.

Ways to deal with labour

Positions for labour and birth

Use a birthing ball, mats and beanbags to try different positions. This can help your baby move down the pelvis. See page 118.

Breathing and relaxation techniques

Practice breathing exercises and relaxation techniques during pregnancy. These are a great way to relieve stress. See page 122.

Bath or shower

Water encourages relaxation and can make the contractions or birth seem less painful. It decreases pressure on your tummy muscles. Water relaxes the perineum (the area of skin between your vagina and your anus or back passage). Some hospitals may have birthing pools but a bath or shower can help too.

Aromatherapy and alternative therapies

Aromatherapy oils can be used in massage, in the bath, on a tissue or by diffuser. These may increase relaxation and reduce pain. Women with asthma or other allergies may not be able to use these oils.

Other options include hypnosis (hypnobirth), yoga, acupuncture or reflexology. These may not be offered in your maternity hospital or unit but may be available privately.

Talk to your midwife if you are considering any alternative methods of pain relief like the above. Most maternity units do not provide these services but may accommodate you.

TENS machine

The word TENS stands for transcutaneous electrical nerve stimulation. This involves passing a gentle electrical current through flat pads on your back. It works better if started early.

You tape the electrodes to your back. These are connected to a small battery-operated stimulator. You can hold this and give yourself small doses of electric current.

The small electric current may stimulate the body to produce endorphins. Endorphins are natural painkillers. Check if your maternity unit supplies TENS machines. If not, they can be rented.

Gas and air (Entonox)

You can be given gas to help with labour pain. The gas is half nitrous oxide and half oxygen. The name of the gas is Entonox. You breathe the gas through a mouthpiece. You should start breathing it as soon as the contraction begins.

The gas can be used at any time, and you are in control. It may make you feel a little dizzy.

Pethidine

Pethidine is a strong painkiller. It is a similar drug to morphine and a type of opioid. Pethidine is an injection given into your leg or bottom. It may help reduce your pain, especially if used alongside other methods.

The injection may make your feel drowsy, dizzy or sick. If given too close to delivery it may mean that baby is a bit sleepy after birth.

Epidural

An epidural is a local anaesthetic. You will have a drip put into your arm beforehand.

You will then have a very small tube inserted in your back by an anaesthetist. Pain-relieving drugs come through the tube once it is in the right place.

The midwife will need to check your blood pressure regularly as sometimes this can fall.

It can usually take away all of your pain and has minimal effect on your baby. Taking an epidural may make the labour longer and reduce your urge to bear down.

It may make it difficult to pass urine (wee). If you have difficulty weeing, you will need a tube inserted into your bladder. This is called a catheter.

1 in 100 women develop a severe headache after an epidural. This can be treated.

Keep an open mind

Bear in mind:

- You may need less or more medication than you had planned
- Your obstetrician or midwife may suggest a particular form of pain relief to help with the labour or birth

Staying active during labour

Being active in labour can distract you from any discomfort you may be feeling. It can also shorten the length of your labour.

You may feel the urge to stay upright and to move around. Listen to your body.

Being upright means using any position other than lying flat.

Benefits of staying upright rather than lying down

Gravity will help your baby move down the birth passage. Pregnant women who are upright and active need less pain relief or interventions to get the baby out.

Better contractions and less pain

When you are upright, your womb tilts forward during labour. This means you will have better contractions and less pain.

Contractions are stronger and more effective when you are upright. This could mean your labour is shorter.

Wider birth canal

The lower part of your spine (sacrum) can move better when you are upright. This means the birth canal can widen and make room for your baby's head. Pelvic joints can expand and move which means less pressure on nerves.

Better for the baby

Your baby may get a better oxygen supply. They may get into a better position for birth.

Did you know?

Walking in labour may help to shorten the early phase of labour. When labour is more established, you might need support to walk between contractions.

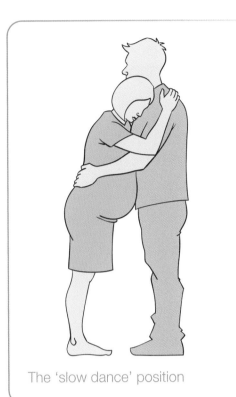

The 'slow dance' position

The 'slow dance' position

The 'slow dance' is a childbirth position that may help. Put your arms around your birth partner's neck and shoulders. Your birth partner can apply counter pressure to any particular spot, or simply hold you. You can rock backwards and forwards. Music may help.

Ways to stay upright during labour

- standing
- sitting on a chair
- on a birthing ball
- kneeling
- squatting
- on all fours

Your movement during labour could be limited by:

- an epidural
- drips (intravenous lines or infusions)
- electronic monitors

Ask your birth partner and midwife to help you change position to stay as comfortable as possible.

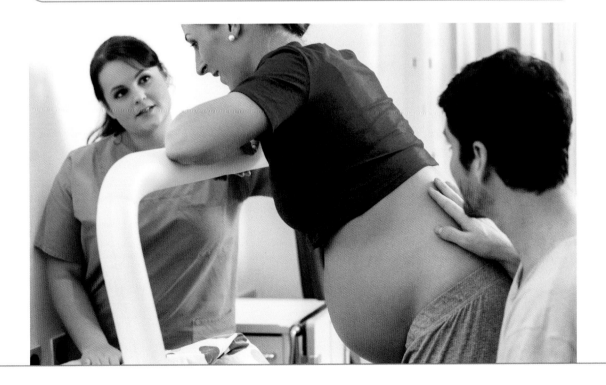

Equipment you can use

Using special equipment during labour can make you feel more comfortable. Practice with this equipment during your pregnancy. Getting used to equipment means you will feel confident using it when you go into labour.

Birthing balls and peanut balls are two types of equipment used during labour.

Birthing ball

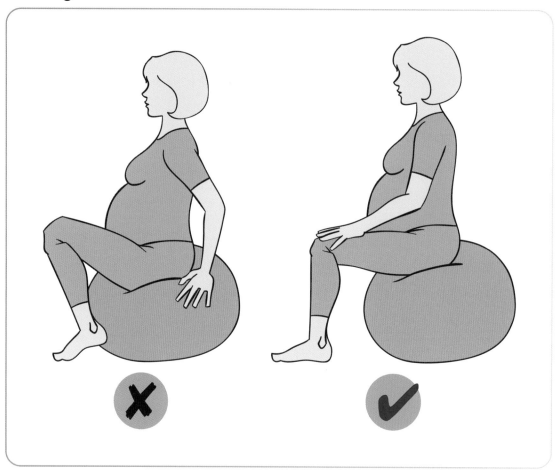

Sitting on a birthing ball can be a comfortable position when you are 'resting' during labour. It helps gravity to assist the birth of your baby. It also allows your birth partner to do some massage if you would like that.

When sitting on a birthing ball, make sure it is inflated such that your hips are higher than your knees. This makes it easier to lean forward to widen your pelvis. Rocking back and forth can be soothing and helps your cervix stretch.

Get a ball with an anti-burst valve. Sometimes pumps are sold with the ball or the ball can be inflated at the air pump at a petrol station.

What size is right for me?

Check your height below to make sure you buy the right size ball. You may need to get a larger ball than the one listed for your height if you have heavy proportions or particularly long legs.

Your height (feet and inches)	Recommended ball size
4 foot 8 inches	45 cm or 18 inches
4 foot 8 inches to 5 foot 3 inches	55 cm or 22 inches
5 foot 4 inches to 5 foot 10 inches	65cm or 26 inches
5 foot 11 inches to 6 foot 4 inches	75cm or 30 inches
6 foot 4 inches and over	85cm or 34 inches

Peanut ball

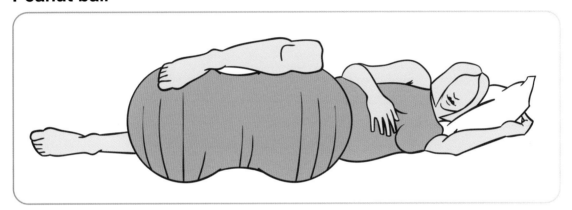

A peanut ball is oval in shape and narrower in the middle.

You may use a peanut ball if you need to remain in the bed, due to epidural use, tiredness or other medical reasons.

The ball is usually placed between the legs to open your pelvis. You can be in a semi-reclined position with one leg over the ball and one leg to the side of the ball. Another recommended position is lying on your side with the ball in between your legs.

Some research shows that women who use a peanut ball have a shorter labour. They are less likely to need a caesarean birth. It is thought that using the ball may help a baby's head rotate into the best position for passing through the birth canal.

These balls come in different sizes, so it is important to try them before buying. For most women, a 45 to 50 cm ball is appropriate. You may prefer a 40 cm ball if you are very petite.

Breathing and self-help techniques

Learning the art of relaxation will help you during pregnancy and labour. It may also help you with the transition to parenthood.

Practising breathing exercises during your pregnancy can be a great way of relieving stress. It will also help you to respond to discomfort during labour.

Developing a relaxed state of mind takes practice.

Breathing techniques

Focusing on your breathing requires you to concentrate. Focused breathing means that your thought process is directed away from any discomfort you may be feeling. This can help during a contraction.

It helps reduce tension in your muscles. This may ease the birthing process. It may also help you to deal with any stress, anxiety or anger that you may be feeling. It reverses some of the physical symptoms of anxiety.

How to do focused breathing

1. Practice taking deep slow breaths from your abdomen (stomach area).
2. Rest your hands at the bottom of your ribs, so that your fingertips are touching.
3. Your fingertips should move apart slightly as you breathe in, and then come together again as your lungs empty.
4. Breathe slowly, for example for a count of 5.
5. Breathe out slowly, as this ensures the diaphragm is pulling air into the bases of the lungs.

Work with your body

Contractions during labour are important. They are a positive force. By listening to your body, you will know what positions work best for you, how to move and how to breathe.

Endorphins

Every contraction is bringing your baby closer to you.

As your contractions get stronger, your body will produce pain-relieving chemicals known as endorphins.

Labour starts a sequence of events in your body. Your body produces hormones to help you bond with your baby and to breastfeed.

You are strong. Your body was designed for labour.

Thinking positive thoughts can help reduce feelings of discomfort and may make you feel more confident.

Examples of positive affirmations (thoughts):

- I am doing well.
- My body was designed for this.
- I am strong and healthy; labour is normal.
- My body and my baby are working together for a safe birth.
- Each surge that I feel is bringing me closer to holding my baby in my arms.

The birth

The next phase of labour involves breathing out your baby. This begins when the cervix (the neck of your womb) is fully dilated (opened) to 10 cm. You are ready to give birth.

Your midwife or obstetrician will guide you through this part of labour. Soon you will be meeting your baby for the very first time.

Find a birth position

During your pregnancy, practice different positions and see what feels comfortable.

Different positions include:

- standing
- kneeling on your knees
- squatting
- kneeling and hugging your birth partner
- lying on your side
- kneeling on all fours
- lying in bed propped up on pillows.

Water births

If you are having a water birth, you may feel more comfortable in positions where the water is covering you. You will also be able to use the sides of the birthing pool for support. This may give you more options to try different positions. Your midwife will support you. They and your birth partner can help you find the position that feels most comfortable.

Breathing out and pushing

Once your cervix is open, you may feel the urge to push. You should work with your body at the start of a contraction.

1. Take a deep breath in.
2. When you breathe out, push down, into your bottom, as if you were trying to have a large bowel movement (poo).

3. Take a breath when you need to and push again.
4. Give several pushes until the contraction ends.
5. Rest between contractions.
6. Your midwife will advise you when to stop pushing

Every birth is different, just as every mother and baby are different.

You may have practiced a different method with your midwife or physiotherapist during your pregnancy. Use whatever technique feels more comfortable to you.

Your midwife is there to support and guide you.

Birthing your baby

Soon your baby's head will move down, and the midwife will see it.

> The midwife will ask you to stop pushing and to pant or blow a few short quick breaths. Practice this before your due date. This is to allow your baby's head to be born slowly and gently.
>
> The skin around the birth passage usually stretches well. Occasionally it can tear. Panting and blowing helps to prevent this.
>
> Once your baby's head is born, give one small and gentle push for the body.
>
> Your baby can be lifted directly onto your tummy or chest if this is what you would like. This is the start of safe skin-to-skin contact.
>
> The umbilical cord will be clamped and cut by your midwife, obstetrician or birth partner.

Birthing the placenta (afterbirth)

After your baby is born, your uterus (womb) can contract to push out the placenta (afterbirth).

Your midwife may offer you an injection to help speed this process up.

This injection is of a drug called syntocinon. The injection reduces the risk of severe bleeding after the birth (post-partum haemorrhage). It also reduces your risk of needing a blood transfusion. This is the method recommended by most obstetricians and midwives.

Some pregnant women who have had straightforward pregnancies and births choose not to have the syntocinon injection.

Your midwife or obstetrician will usually support your choice. But if they feel you are at high risk of having a bleed, they will advise you to get the injection.

Your midwife and obstetrician will discuss the risks and benefits to help you make an informed choice.

Breastfeeding as soon as possible will also help your womb contract.

When nature needs a hand

Some babies need a little help to be born. There are a few medical procedures that may be needed to start off your labour or to help your baby be born.

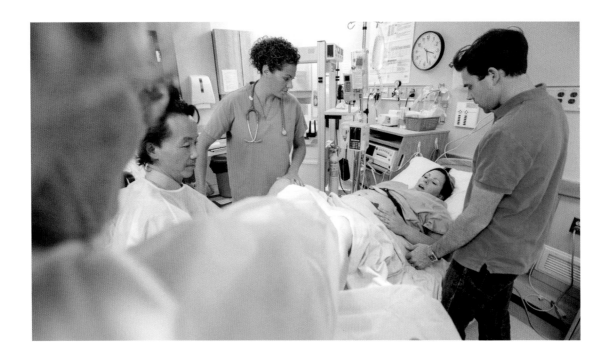

When a procedure is recommended, never be afraid to ask questions.

- Why do I need this?
- What could happen if this is not done?
- Are there any risks to me from this procedure?
- What are the alternatives?

Inducing (starting off) labour

'Induction' of labour describes ways that may be used to start your labour. This is generally needed if:

- your baby is overdue
- your waters have broken but labour has not started
- the health of you or your baby is at risk

There are many ways of inducing labour.

Prostaglandin gel

This is a hormonal gel that is inserted into the vagina. It encourages the cervix to soften and open. It can take up to 72 hours to work. Once labour starts, it should continue normally.

Membrane sweep

Membrane sweeping involves your midwife or obstetrician putting a gloved finger inside your vagina until it reaches your cervix (the neck of your womb). They will place their fingertip just inside your cervix and make a circular movement. This may stimulate your cervix to produce hormones that may trigger labour.

Artificial rupture of membranes

Occasionally your midwife or doctor will need to break your waters. This is called an 'amniotomy'.

The membranes may be ruptured using a specialised tool, such as an amnihook or amnicot. They may also be ruptured by the obstetrician's finger.

Balloons

Labour can be induced by placing a small tube with a small balloon on the end of it in the neck of the womb. This method avoids any risk of too many contractions.

Oxytocin

The body produces a hormone called oxytocin in labour. Sometimes you will need synthetic oxytocin during labour. This to induce your labour or to make your contractions more regular.

> One of the main risks of having your labour induced is that the contractions could become more frequent. Too many contractions can harm your baby. You are entitled to information about this. Do not be afraid to ask for extra information.

Episiotomy

This is not routinely done. An episiotomy is a small cut to make the opening of the vagina bigger. It is sometimes done to speed up the birth of the baby's head.

The cut is usually made in the perineum. This is the area between the vagina and back passage. You will need stitches afterwards.

Practicing perineal massage (page 104) during pregnancy may reduce your chances of needing an episiotomy.

Stitches

Small grazes and tears will not require stitches. If you have a larger tear or an episiotomy you may need stitches. Normally you will be holding your baby in safe skin to skin as this is being done. If you have an epidural, this can be topped up before the stitches are done, otherwise you will be given some local anaesthetic.

Assisted births: forceps and ventouse (vacuum)

An assisted birth is when forceps or a ventouse suction cup are used to help deliver the baby.

Situations where assistance may be needed:

- If you have been pushing for a long time with no sign of imminent birth.
- When an immediate birth is needed for your baby's safety.

Ventouse

A ventouse is a suction cup. It is fitted to your baby's head. As you push, the obstetrician will guide your baby's head along the birth canal.

Forceps

Forceps are spoon-shaped instruments. They are curved to cradle your baby's head. Forceps are used to guide your baby's head through the birth canal as you push.

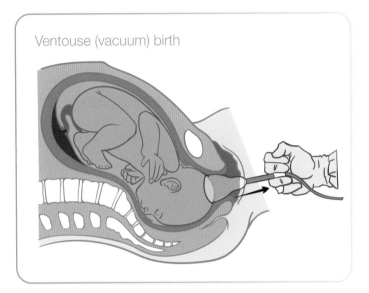

Ventouse (vacuum) birth

Caesarean birth

In a caesarean birth your baby is born through a cut in your abdomen (tummy). It is also known as a 'C-section'. A caesarean birth takes place in an operating theatre.

Some caesarean births are planned. Others are emergency caesarean births, when complications happen during labour.

Reasons for caesareans

The most common reasons for an emergency caesarean:

- Labour is not progressing.
- The baby needs to be born quickly.

The most common reasons for an elective (planned) caesarean:

- Your baby remains in the breech position.
- You have a low-lying placenta (placenta praevia).

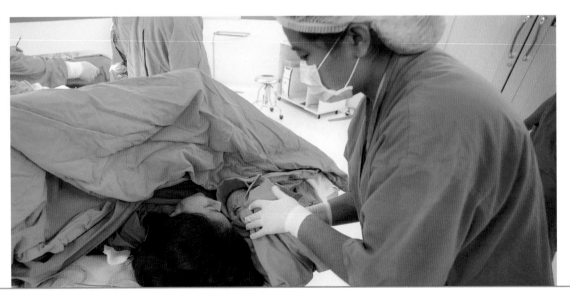

What happens during a caesarean

A spinal anaesthetic or epidural is used in most caesarean births. This means you are awake during the operation and do not feel any pain.

Birth partner

Your birth partner will wear a gown and mask if they attend the birth. They may have to wait outside until the operation has started.

If you have a general anaesthetic, your birth partner will normally not be allowed into the operating theatre. They can wait close by and will be updated as soon as there is news.

How long it takes

The entire procedure takes around 45 minutes. It can be quicker or slower depending on the circumstances. Usually your baby will be born in 5 to 10 minutes.

When the baby is born

Your baby may be checked by a paediatric doctor (a doctor specialising in children's health). Your midwife will help you and your partner to have safe skin-to-skin contact.

Recovering from a caesarean

You may feel uncomfortable after a caesarean.

You will be:

- offered pain-relieving medication
- have a drip in your arm to give you fluids
- usually be in hospital for 3 to 4 days

Catheter

A tube called a catheter will be in your bladder. It is inserted at the time of the operation and left in for approximately 24 hours afterwards. Catheters are used to drain wee out of your bladder until you can go to the toilet yourself.

Injections into your abdominal wall (tummy)

You will usually receive injections into your stomach (tummy) to prevent blood clots.

Everyday tasks

You may have to wait a few hours after your caesarean operation before you are allowed to eat anything. You will be helped to shower the next day, and encouraged to be mobile as soon as possible. A chartered physiotherapist who specialises in women's health may see you to help your recovery.

Usually you will not be allowed to drive for up to six weeks after a caesarean birth.

Your newborn baby

The first glimpse of your baby

You may have visualised a cute baby with chubby cheeks and wonderful gurgling noises. Your baby will be beautiful, but their first appearance may be a little surprising. Newborns are often wet, wrinkled and red with an unusually long or pointed head!

Initial examination of your baby

Immediately after birth, your midwife or paediatrician will examine your baby. This is to see if you have had a boy or a girl. They will also look for any visible health problems that need immediate action.

Vitamin K injection

Most doctors, nurses and midwives recommend that all newborn babies get a vitamin K injection. This is to help their blood to clot and prevent bleeding disorders. You'll need to give your consent for this. Your baby will then get the injection immediately after birth.

It is a small injection into your baby's thigh. There are no reported side-effects, but occasionally babies can have redness or swelling around the site of injection.

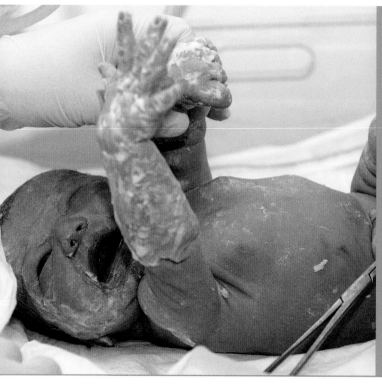

Normal variations in the appearance of newborns

Newborns can vary in their appearance. Some of the normal variations include:

Colour	Brand new babies often have a dark red or purple appearance. This begins to fade over a few days.
Vernix	This is a white greasy substance. It covers the skin of many newborn babies, especially in skin folds.
Moulding	This is when a newborn baby's head has a long shape. It is caused by bones overlapping in your baby's skull to help pass through the birth canal. The head returns to a more normal shape after one week.
Skin	Many babies born on or after their due dates may have dry and scaly skin. Some newborns have a red rash on their chest and back. This is known as 'erythema toxicum'. It will disappear after a few days.
Lanugo	Some babies are born with soft, downy hair all over their bodies. This is more common in premature babies.
Milia or 'milk spots'	These are tiny white and hard spots on a baby's nose. They look like pimples. These are caused by oil glands and will disappear on their own.
Mongolian spots	These are blue or purple spots, also known as 'Mongolian Blue spots'. They usually appear on your baby's lower back or buttocks. They can sometimes appear in other places like your baby's arms or legs. Most of the time, this discolouration disappears without any treatment by age 4, but occasionally it can last for longer. Mongolian spots are more common in dark-skinned babies.

Bonding with your baby

Skin-to-skin contact

For most babies, skin-to-skin contact is just what they need to calm them and warm them after birth.

During skin-to-skin contact, you and your baby will produce a hormone called oxytocin. This helps you feel close to your baby.

After the birth

Immediately after the birth, a midwife will dry your baby and place them on your chest. Your baby will be naked (except for a hat and nappy). You will get a blanket to keep you and your baby warm.

Enjoy this time, rest and relax together. This is your chance to get to know your baby, to look at tiny fingers, toes and their nose!

Birth partner's skin-to-skin contact

Your birth partner can also take part in skin-to-skin contact to bond with the baby. If you or your baby are unable to try skin-to-skin contact after birth, for whatever reason, don't worry. You can have these moments at a later stage when you are both ready.

Signs of wanting to feed

During this time, your baby may start showing signs of wanting to feed. They may move towards your breast, or you may need to help them. They will try to latch or attach to your breast. Keep your baby skin-to-skin during this first feed and afterwards, for as long as you wish.

Watch your baby closely while you are having skin-to-skin. Make sure they have a normal breathing pattern and that their skin colour does not change.

Benefits of skin-to-skin contact for your baby

Skin-to-skin contact helps your baby:

- stay warm
- feel less stress from being born
- adjust to life outside the womb
- stabilise their breathing
- regulate their blood sugar
- get protection from the 'good bacteria' that pass from skin to their skin – this helps protects against infection

---

"You are my universe. I could pick you out in a crowd."

Building a relationship with your baby

Responsive parenting is an important part of forming a healthy relationship with your baby. It means that you are responding to your baby while accepting their needs and signals.

This type of parenting helps your baby form healthy brain connections and encourages feelings of safety and comfort.

Tips to help with responsive parenting

Hold them close

Your baby loves when you hold them close. It comforts your baby and helps them feel secure.

Too young for routines

Newborn babies are not able to learn routines. A newborn baby does not know the difference between day and night. They also have very small stomachs, and need to feed little and often. It is normal for newborn babies to need to feed several times during the night. As your baby grows, they will gradually sleep for longer between feeds. This hopefully should mean less night awakenings!

Body language

Your baby will let you know in their own little ways what they need. It will take time to learn what your baby is trying to tell you.

For example, your baby loves you speaking or singing to them but when they get tired they will turn away or rub their eyes. Soon you will learn to read these signals and know that your baby needs a break.

Responding to their needs

Remember, you are not 'spoiling' your baby by responding to their needs.

Bonding with your body

During pregnancy, your body worked very hard. You managed to grow an entire human being from one tiny cell!

Just as it took time to grow your pregnancy, it will take time for your body to recover from pregnancy. Be patient and kind to yourself.

Common issues after pregnancy

After pains

After your baby is born, you may feel painful period-like cramps in your stomach. This happens as your uterus (womb) returns to the size it was before pregnancy.

These cramps should go away after a few days. Your midwife or obstetrician will examine you to check that the womb is shrinking.

You may feel these pains are more severe when you breastfeed. Breastfeeding stimulates your womb to contract to normal. Ask your midwife or obstetrician about what painkillers you can take to help with this.

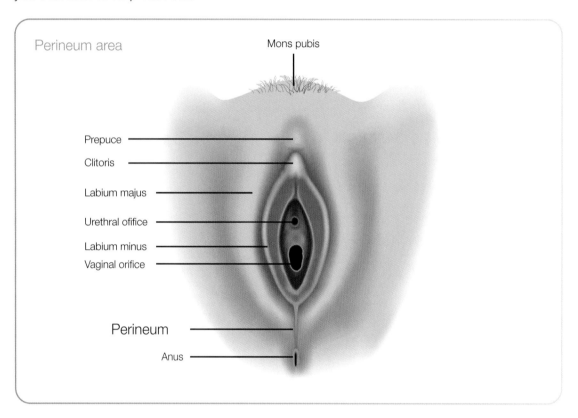

Perineum area

Mons pubis

Prepuce

Clitoris

Labium majus

Urethral ofifice

Labium minus

Vaginal orifice

Perineum

Anus

Perineum area

Your perineum is the area of skin between the back of your vagina and your anus (back passage). During labour and birth, this area of skin stretches and may even tear.

After giving birth, this area may be sore and swollen. If you have had stitches, this area may feel particularly tender.

You will need to take care of the perineum. You should:

- change your pads frequently
- wash your hands (before and after changing pads)
- have a bath or shower each day to keep the perineal area clean
- do your pelvic floor exercises

> Call your midwife or GP if the wound becomes open or starts to ooze green or smelly fluid.

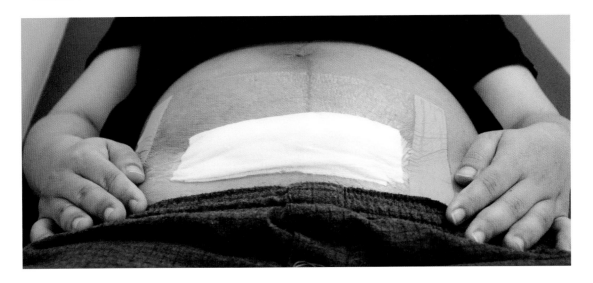

Changes following a caesarean birth

A caesarean birth is major surgery, so it will take time to recover. You will need extra rest. The blood you lost during surgery may mean that you feel very tired.

Your wound can be quite uncomfortable. Talk to your obstetrician, GP or midwife about medications to help you feel more comfortable. Enlist your partner, family and friends to help you as you recover.

Vaginal discharge or bleeding (lochia)

After giving birth, it is normal for bloody fluid to discharge from your vagina for up to 6 weeks. This is called lochia. It is your body's way of getting rid of the extra blood and tissue that was in your womb during pregnancy.

Colour of blood

The colour of the blood flow is bright red at first. This will change to brown and eventually to a yellow or whitish colour as the uterus heals.

Changes to the blood

It is normal to see an increase in the amount or a darkening in the colour of the blood if you do something physically tiring. This may be a sign that you need to take it easy.

What to do

Do not use a tampon. You can use a maternity pad or a sanitary towel.

> Call your midwife, public health nurse or GP if:
>
> - the bleeding becomes heavy with clots
> - or it starts to have a foul-smell

Bladder and bowel problems

Some women may have difficulty controlling urine (wee) or faeces (poo) after childbirth. You may notice urine or poo is leaking.

Contact your GP, public health nurse or physiotherapist if your symptoms are not improving after 6 weeks after the birth.

Stinging when passing urine

You may have some pain or stinging when you pass urine for a few days. Drink plenty of fluids.

Constipation

Some women have trouble having a bowel movement (a poo) after giving birth.

Drink lots of fluids like water and eat foods that are high in fibre.

Talk to your GP or midwife if you go more than 3 days without a bowel movement.

> High-fibre foods include oats, wholegrain bread and pasta, fruit and vegetables, potatoes with their skin on, peas, beans and legumes.

Piles (haemorrhoids)

Haemorrhoids are painful swollen veins around the back passage. These may get worse after giving birth.

Drink plenty of fluids and eat foods rich in fibre. Talk to your GP about medications.

Pelvic organ prolapse

Prolapse can happen when there is a weakness in structures which support your pelvic floor. This weakness allows one or more of the pelvic organs to move down into the walls of the vagina. The womb, bowel or bladder bulges into the vagina.

The pelvic floor is usually weak after pregnancy and childbirth. Contact your GP, public health nurse or physiotherapist if you think you have symptoms of prolapse.

Some symptoms of prolapse include:

- a dragging pain in your vagina or lower tummy
- seeing or feeling a bulge in your vagina or the sensation of 'something coming down'

Sex after pregnancy

Sex after pregnancy may be difficult and painful for women. If you have had a perineal tear or an episiotomy, this can make sex painful at first.

You may also find your desire to have sex changes, particularly if you are exhausted or feeling low. This is normal. Talking to your partner about how you feel is important.

Breast changes

Your breasts will get bigger and more firm. They will produce the first milk called colostrum. This is a yellow colour.

Your milk then changes to a more white colour. Your breasts will make more milk about 3 days after the birth of your baby.

Hair loss

Your hair may have seemed thicker and fuller during pregnancy. It is common for hair to thin out after the baby has been born. You may even lose hair.

Eat plenty of fruit and vegetables. Be gentle with your hair.

Remember

Your body is amazing, it kept your baby safe.

Feeding your baby

Breastfeeding – getting started

Most babies are alert and keen to breastfeed soon after birth, but every baby is different. Follow your baby's feeding cues. Your nurse or midwife is there to help and support you.

Colostrum

Every pregnant woman has milk ready for her baby at birth. This is known as colostrum. It is sometimes called 'liquid gold'.

It is produced in small amounts by your body and is quite thick in consistency.

Colostrum is full of antibodies that will help your baby fight off infection. Every breastfeed makes a difference.

The first few days

How often

A newborn baby can feed 10 to 12 times in 24 hours. In the early days, breastfeeding takes patience and practice.

It is important to breastfeed your baby early and often. Every time your baby feeds, they are letting your body know how much breast milk you need to produce.

Feed your baby as often as they want. This will help you stay comfortable.

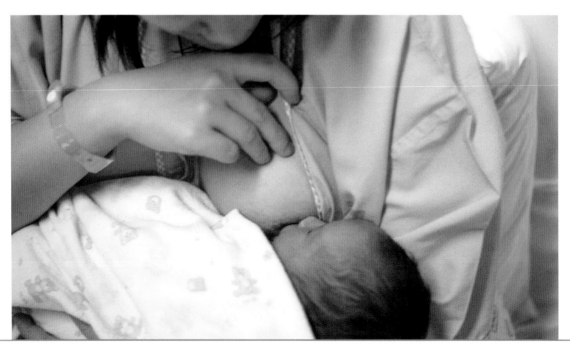

'Milk coming in'

You may notice your breasts are beginning to make more milk and becoming fuller and firmer. This happens at some point from day 2 to 4. It is sometimes known as 'your milk coming in'.

Leaks

Sometimes breast milk may leak from your nipples. If you use breast pads, change them regularly or at every feed.

Signs your baby is hungry

Early feeding cues

Signs your baby is hungry are called early feeding cues. They include:

- eyes fluttering
- moving their hands to their mouth
- making mouth movements
- moving towards your breast or turning their head when you touch their cheek

Crying

Crying is a late sign of hunger or late feeding cue. Try feeding when your baby gives you the earlier signs.

It will often be easier as you will both be calmer and more relaxed.

Breastfeeding positions

You can breastfeed in a number of different positions. Find one that is comfortable for both of you.

Remember to keep your baby safe at all times. Have a drink close to hand, and perhaps a snack. Like any new skill, breastfeeding takes practice.

See mychild.ie for step-by-step guides on different breastfeeding positions you can try.

Breastfeeding: positioning and attachment

Positioning and attachment is about how you hold your baby at your breast so they can feed. This is sometimes called 'latching on'. When your baby is well positioned and attached, they will find it easier to feed well and you will find it more comfortable.

In the early days, you may feel sensitive at the beginning of a feed as you get used to the new feeling. Feeding should not be painful.

How to position and attach

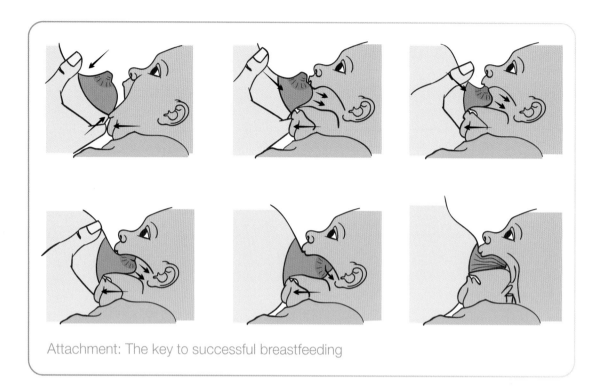

Attachment: The key to successful breastfeeding

Follow these steps to position and attach your baby well:

1. Hold your baby close with their nose level with your nipple.
2. Let your baby's head tip back so their top lip brushes against your nipple – this should help them open their mouth wide.
3. When your baby's mouth is wide open, bring them to your breast.
4. Aim your nipple to the roof of their mouth.
5. When they attach, your nipple and most of the areola (the area around your nipple) should be deep in your baby's mouth.
6. When your baby is attached properly, their chin will be pressed into your breast.
7. Your baby's nose should be clear for easy breathing.
8. If your baby's nose appears to be blocked, move their bottom closer to you. This will create a head tilt and free up their nose.
9. The deeper the attachment, the more comfortable you will feel and the better your baby will feed.
10. More of your areola will be visible above their top lip than below their bottom lip.
11. Their cheeks will appear fuller.
12. They'll suck quickly at first, followed by longer sucks.
13. You will hear them swallowing.

Guidelines for mothers

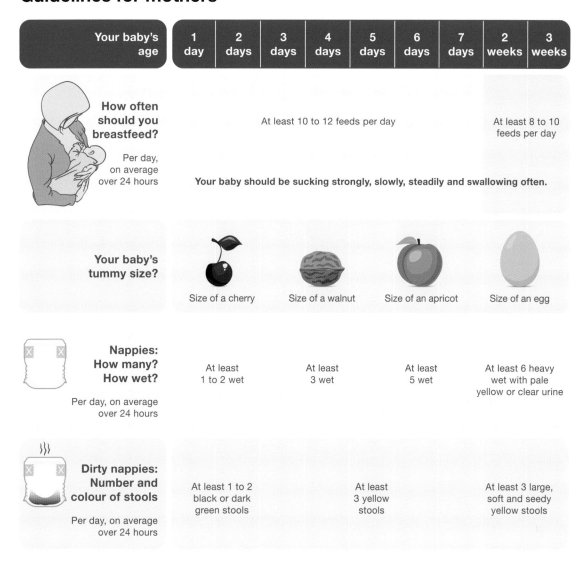

Your baby's age	1 day	2 days	3 days	4 days	5 days	6 days	7 days	2 weeks	3 weeks
How often should you breastfeed? Per day, on average over 24 hours	At least 10 to 12 feeds per day							At least 8 to 10 feeds per day	
	Your baby should be sucking strongly, slowly, steadily and swallowing often.								
Your baby's tummy size?	Size of a cherry		Size of a walnut		Size of an apricot			Size of an egg	
Nappies: How many? How wet? Per day, on average over 24 hours	At least 1 to 2 wet		At least 3 wet		At least 5 wet			At least 6 heavy wet with pale yellow or clear urine	
Dirty nappies: Number and colour of stools Per day, on average over 24 hours	At least 1 to 2 black or dark green stools				At least 3 yellow stools			At least 3 large, soft and seedy yellow stools	

How do I know my baby is getting enough?

Newborn babies have small stomachs. It might seem you are only producing a small amount of colostrum. However, this is more than enough to fill a tiny tummy.

What goes in, must come out! Your baby's nappies will help you to see if they are getting enough breast milk.

Your baby should be producing wet and dirty nappies. Your baby's first dirty nappies are black and tarry. This is called meconium.

Over the next day or so, your baby's poos become greenish in colour. By day 5, your baby will have yellow seedy poos.

Day	Wet nappies	Dirty nappies
1	1 wet nappy or more (over 24 hours)	1 stool (black) or more
2	2 wet nappies or more	2 stools (black) or more
3	3 wet nappies or more	3 stools (black or greenish) or more
4	4 wet nappies or more	3 to 4 stools (greenish or yellowish) or more
5	5 wet nappies or more	Stools should turn yellow
6 days to 6 weeks	6 wet nappies or more (heavy and wet with pale, yellow or clear urine)	3 to 8 stools or more (yellow, seedy, runny to loose) daily

Other signs your baby is getting enough breast milk:

Your baby:

- has a strong cry
- is active and alert
- is waking easily
- is satisfied and content after many feeds

Your breasts should feel softer after feeds.

Did you know?

It's normal for babies lose weight in the first few days after birth. After this they begin gaining weight and by 2 weeks of age they usually are back at their birth weight.

Common breastfeeding questions

Does breastfeeding hurt?

In the early weeks, some mothers say they feel tenderness at the beginning of a breastfeed. You need to get help if soreness continues during the feed. See page 146.

The main reason may be:

- your baby is not positioned correctly on your breast, or
- a different breastfeeding position might suit better

Get help from your midwife, neonatal nurse, public health nurse, or your lactation consultant. You can get advice from lactation consultants on mychild.ie

Changing position

If a position doesn't feel right, take your baby off the breast and start again. Slide one of your fingers into your baby's mouth to gently break the suction before taking them off the breast.

Always wash your hands carefully before you begin breastfeeding your baby.

What if my breasts feel sore and full?

If your breasts become very full in the first few days, this may feel uncomfortable. Tips include:

Feed often

Feeding your baby will ease the full feeling. The more often you feed your baby, the more comfortable you will feel.

Warm your breasts

Warm your breasts with a warm facecloth or in the shower if:

- your breasts are very uncomfortable
- your baby is finding it hard to attach

This will help your milk to flow.

Hand express before a feed

Hand expressing some breast milk before the feed can also help. This will soften your breast and help your baby attach onto your breast.

Can I use a soother?

Try not to give your baby a soother, dummy or dodie until breastfeeding is established. This means that your supply of breast milk matches your baby's needs. Breastfeeding works by supply and demand. The more you breastfeed, the more milk your body produces. Breastfeeding takes a number of weeks to get established.

Using soothers has been shown to reduce the amount of breast milk your body makes. It may also interfere with your baby attaching correctly onto your breast.

Do I need a special diet?

There's no need to follow a special diet when you are breastfeeding. Breastfeeding is thirsty work so make sure you are drinking plenty of water.

Being a new mother is busy and can be hard work. Try to have a healthy and balanced diet to make sure you are getting all of the nutrients you need.

A healthy and balanced diet means:

- at least 5 to 7 servings of vegetables, salad and fruit each day
- wholegrain bread, pasta, rice or potatoes
- plenty of fibre to prevent constipation – wholegrains, beans, lentils, fruit and vegetables
- protein such as lean meat, poultry, fish and eggs
- dairy foods such as milk, cheese and yoghurts

Top tip:
Try to have healthy snacks ready to grab for when you get hungry.

Examples of healthy snacks are:

- fresh fruit
- yoghurts
- hummus and vegetables to dip in like carrots and celery
- sandwiches
- dried fruit like mangoes, apricots and prunes
- breakfast cereals or muesli that are fortified with vitamins
- baked beans on toast
- baked potato with cheese
- boiled eggs

Do I need to avoid certain things?

Alcohol

Avoid drinking alcohol in the first month after your baby is born. This is because it is difficult to predict when a newborn baby might need to breastfeed. Alcohol could be present in small amounts in your breast milk.

It is safe to drink alcohol and breastfeed after the first month if you:

- feed your baby and express breastmilk before drinking
- wait 2 hours after each standard drink before breastfeeding your baby
- have a limit of 11 standard drinks a week
- spread your drinks over the week
- have at least 2 alcohol-free days per week

1 standard drink is a half a pint of beer, a single measure of spirits or a small glass of wine.

Caffeine

Drinks containing caffeine like tea, coffee and energy drinks may keep your baby awake. Keep your caffeine intake to less than 200 mg per day, the same as when you were pregnant.

Examples of caffeine containing foods and drinks include:

- 1 mug of filter coffee – 140 mg caffeine
- 1 mug of instant coffee – 100 mg caffeine
- 1 mug of tea – 75 mg caffeine
- 1 can of energy drank can have up to 160 mg caffeine, depending on the size
- 1 cola drink tends to have 40 mg caffeine

Foods to avoid

Oily fish contains special types of fats. These are called long chain omega fatty acids. These fats are really good for your baby's developing nervous system. But some oily fish can contain low levels of pollutants. These can build up in the body.

If you are breastfeeding, don't have more than two portions of oily fish per week. You should not eat more than one portion of marlin, swordfish or shark per week. This is because these fish can contain high levels of mercury. There is no limit to how much tuna you can eat, as long as you are not pregnant.

Medication

Make sure any medicine, tablets or pills you take are safe for breastfeeding. Check with your GP, any doctor who is treating you or your pharmacist.

How long should I breastfeed for?

Once you and your baby have learned the skill of breastfeeding, it becomes easier every day.

Every day of breastfeeding makes a positive difference for your baby. You don't need to decide at the start how long you will continue.

The first 6 months

Exclusive breastfeeding with no other foods or drinks is recommended for the first 6 months of your baby's life.

After 6 months

After the first 6 months, your baby will start eating other foods and drinks. You can continue giving them breast milk for as long as you want.

What about breastfeeding more than one baby?

Twin, triplets and even more can be breastfed! As these babies may have been born small or early, breastfeeding is even more important for their health.

How to do it

You may find it easier at the start to feed them separately. This will help you to build your confidence.

Triplets can be fed with two together and then one alone, or rotated one by one.

Aim to give as much breast milk as possible to your babies. The amount of breast milk you produce depends on how often and how regularly your babies feed.

Breastfeeding challenges

Breastfeeding is a skill that mothers and babies must learn together. Like any skill, it takes practice and patience.

Things that help to prevent breastfeeding challenges:

- Feed your baby frequently when they show early feeding cues (see page 139).
- Make sure your baby is positioned and attached deeply onto your breast (see page 139).

If you do have any challenges, you are not alone. Ask for help. Almost every breastfeeding problem has a breastfeeding solution!

Sore or bleeding nipples

If your nipples are sore or bleeding, get help.

Ask your neonatal nurse, midwife, public health nurse, GP practice nurse or lactation consultant to check that your baby is correctly positioned and attached to the breast.

They will help you to:

- become more comfortable feeding
- treat sore nipples

If positioning and attachment isn't the cause of the problem, they will advise you about treatment. Other causes may include tongue-tie or thrush.

Tips

If positioning and attachment is the cause, the following tips may help:

- Carefully wash your hands before feeding your baby.
- After each feed, hand express some milk. Gently rub the milk into the nipple area. Let this dry before covering again.
- Gently massage your nipples with warm fingers and 100% lanolin nipple ointment – follow the instructions and make sure you are in a warm room.
- Spread a small amount of 100% lanolin nipple cream on a clean dry breastpad and place over the nipple. Change the breastpad frequently (read the instructions) to prevent moisture staying on your skin.
- Use a hydrogel compress – ask your pharmacist for advice on which is suitable for breastfeeding women and follow the instructions.

If it feels too painful to feed, you could pump milk for a day or two. This gives your nipples time to heal. Hand expressing may be more comfortable than using a pump.

If using a breast pump, start on the lowest setting. Increase it slowly to the lowest setting at which your milk starts to flow well.

Unsettled feeding

Unsettled feeding means your baby is fussing or crying at the breast.

Ask for help from your midwife, neonatal nurse, lactation consultant, GP practice nurse or public health nurse about the best ways to correctly position and attach your baby to your breast. When your baby has finished the first breast, try offering your second breast at each feed.

Engorgement

Breast engorgement is when your breasts get too full of milk. This can leave them feeling hard and painful.

Engorgement can happen in the early days of feeding. It can take a few days for your supply of breast milk to match what your baby needs. It can also happen later on, for example when you introduce solid foods to your baby.

Ask your midwife, neonatal nurse, public health nurse, GP practice nurse or lactation consultant for help if you think your breasts are engorged. They can show you how to express a little milk by hand before a feed to soften your breast and help the baby to attach.

Other tips include:

- Wear a well-fitting bra (nursing bra) designed for breastfeeding mothers.
- Apply warm flannels to your breasts before a feed or before you hand express.
- Keep cabbage leaves in the fridge and put them on your breasts after a feed.
- Ask your nurse or doctor if you can take paracetamol or ibuprofen to help with the pain.

Blocked ducts

If you have a blocked duct, you will usually notice an area of your breast that is sore. You might feel a hard and tender lump when you press your breast. You will generally feel well.

A blocked duct can happen when the milk is not flowing freely from that milk duct in your breast. Causes can include wearing a bra that is too tight, incorrect positioning and attachment or missing a feed.

Mastitis

Mastitis means you have an inflammation in one of your breasts. This can happen when a blocked duct is not relieved. If mastitis is not treated, it can become infected and you will need to take antibiotics.

If you have mastitis, you may have:

- a red patch of skin on your breast that is painful to touch
- a high fever
- flu-like symptoms – feeling generally unwell, achy and tired. You may feel tearful too.

Ask your midwife, public health nurse or lactation consultant to check that your baby is correctly positioned and attached to the breast.

Tips

Some tips to help a blocked duct or mastitis include:

- Feed more often and feed from the affected breast first.
- If your baby cannot feed, express from that side.
- Warm up your breast with a hot wet flannel before feeding.
- If you have mastitis only, cool your breast with a cold facecloth or flannel after the feed.
- Massage your breast while baby is feeding.
- Rest and take a painkiller like paracetamol or ibuprofen (check with your nurse or GP if you can use this medication).

See your GP if there is no improvement after 12 to 24 hours or if things are getting worse.

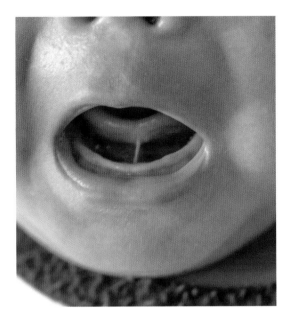

Tongue-tie

Some babies with tongue-tie are not able to move and stretch their tongues freely and this may interfere with positioning and attachment. This can cause feeding challenges. It can also cause problems like nipple pain.

Tongue-tie can reduce the amount of breast milk your baby gets. This can result in poor weight gain. It can also reduce a mother's supply of breast milk.

What to do

See your lactation consultant, public health nurse, neonatal nurse, midwife, GP practice nurse or GP if you think your baby has tongue-tie. There is more information on mychild.ie.

Where to get breastfeeding support

- Your midwife, lactation consultant, public health nurse or GP
- Mychild.ie has a free 'ask the expert' service and webchat for breastfeeding questions and information on local breastfeeding groups
- Cuidiú – cuidiu.ie
- La Leche League – lalecheleagueireland.com
- Friends of Breastfeeding – friendsofbreastfeeding.ie

Breastfeeding out and about

It is lovely to have the convenience of breastfeeding. You can breastfeed your baby anywhere, anytime. There is very little you need to bring with you, just a nappy change.

Building your confidence

Some mothers feel self-conscious breastfeeding out and about the first time, particularly attaching the baby to the breast. This gets easier with time.

Going to a breastfeeding support group and seeing other mothers breastfeeding can help with your confidence.

Try putting a light scarf or muslin cloth over your shoulder to give you some privacy while feeding or attaching your baby on to feed. As you get more comfortable feeding your baby out and about, you won't need these. Some babies don't like to be partially covered, so do what works best for you both. Breastfeeding offers comfort as well as food. That's why breastfed babies are often more easily settled.

Tips for breastfeeding in public

- Bring your partner or a friend along for support until you become more confident.
- Wear a loose top over a vest or cami top so that you can lift up the outer top and pull down the strappy top.
- Wearing a nursing bra helps, as you can quickly click it open and attach your baby on your breast.
- Don't wait until your baby gets too hungry or distressed.

Know your rights

The Equal Status Act (2000) helps mothers to breastfeed comfortably in public places by protecting them from being discriminated against or harassed because they are breastfeeding. Discrimination is unfair treatment. For example, asking someone to leave a premises because they are breastfeeding.

You are entitled to breastfeed in public places and you don't have to ask anyone for permission. Some places may offer a private area if you would like this, but you don't have to use it.

Expressing breast milk

Expressing means removing milk from your breast so you can store it and feed it to your baby later.

You remove the milk by hand or with a breast pump. In the first few days after the birth it is best to hand express. Expressing your breast milk is a very useful skill to learn.

In the early days, you may want to express milk if:

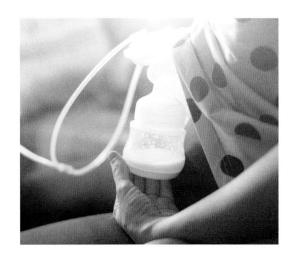

- your baby needs to be cared for in a special care baby unit, neonatal intensive care unit or paediatric hospital
- you or your baby are too ill to breastfeed after birth
- your breasts feel very full or uncomfortable
- your baby is having difficulty attaching on to the breast

As your baby grows, you may want to express milk when you are going to be away from your baby.

Expressing means that during the time you're away from your baby:

- you'll be able to relieve the fullness in your breasts
- you'll have milk for your baby's carer

Did you know?

When you express, it can be helpful to close your eyes and imagine your baby is feeding at your breast.

Thinking of your baby or looking at a photo or video of your baby can help you relax and connect with your baby before you begin expressing. Having their clothing or blanket with you can also help.

If possible, spend some time together in skin-to-skin contact before you begin to express.

Hand-expressing breast milk

Getting ready

- Wash your hands.
- Have everything you need to hand – for example, a drink, snack and a small towel.
- Sit comfortably.
- Think about your baby.
- Warm your breasts – take a warm shower or put a warm facecloth (warm compress) on your breasts
- Massage your breasts before expressing – you can do this while in the shower.

Massaging and expressing

Massage your breasts. This encourages the release of hormones and helps get your milk flowing.

This can be done with your fingertips (as shown in image A) or by rolling your closed fist over your breast towards the nipple (as shown in image B).

1. Work around the whole breast, including underneath. Don't slide your fingers along your breast as it can damage the skin.

2. After massaging your breast, gently roll your nipple between your first finger and thumb (as shown in image C).

3. You can then press and release your breast. Use rhythmic movements. When you press down and release, a small drop of breast milk appears. Do not rub or slide along your nipple as this may hurt.

4. Continue to press and release. After a while, a few drops of breastmilk appears. Collect this in a clean container or syringe. This will be provided by a nurse or midwife if you are in a hospital.

5. Continue then to press, release and collect.

The first milk (colostrum) tends to drip slowly as it is thick, later milk may come in spurts or sprays.

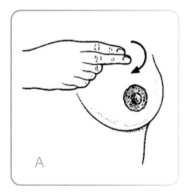
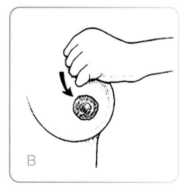
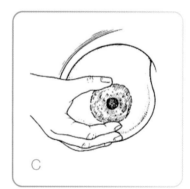

Using a breast pump

If you're regularly separated from your baby or if there is a delay in breastfeeding after birth, your midwife, neonatal nurse or doctor may recommend using a breast pump to express your milk.

You may also need to use a breast pump if your baby is unable to attach onto your breast. For example, if they are too sick, premature or have problems attaching to your breast.

To make sure your breasts make enough milk, you will need to express 8 to 10 times in 24 hours. This includes during the night.

Ask your midwife or neonatal nurse about having skin-to-skin contact (page 131) with your baby as soon as possible after birth.

If your baby is being cared for in a special care baby unit, neonatal intensive care unit or paediatric hospital, they may have hospital grade pumps that you can use free of charge. If you want to use a hospital grade pump while you are at home, you will need to rent or buy one.

You may be able to claim back on any breast pumps you rented or bought for your premature baby through Revenue (see revenue.ie). Use the med 1 form that covers expenses incurred on any medical, surgical or nursing appliance.

Storing expressed breast milk

In the hospital

In the hospital, ask your midwife where your milk can be stored. Make sure to label your name, the date and time on each container.

At home

Use a washed container. Any container will do as long as it has an airtight seal and can be washed or sterilised and labelled easily. You may also choose to use disposable one-use breast milk storage bags.

Label each container with date and time.

You can keep stored milk:

- sealed outside of the fridge for up to 4 hours in temperatures less than 20 degrees
- in a fridge for up to 5 days (place it at the back of the shelf above the vegetable compartment and not inside the door)
- in the icebox in your fridge for up to 2 weeks
- in a fridge freezer for 3 months
- in a deep freezer for up to 6 months

Heating expressed breast milk

When you are expressing, the breast milk should be chilled or frozen as quickly as possible. Follow these guidelines for defrosting or warming up expressed breast milk.

Defrosting frozen milk

Breast milk can be defrosted in the fridge, normally in around 12 hours. Alternatively, hold the bottle or bag of frozen milk under warm running water (a maximum of 37°C or 99°F).

Don't leave frozen breast milk to defrost at room temperature.

Once fully thawed, previously frozen breast milk may be kept at room temperature for a maximum of 2 hours or in the fridge for up to 24 hours.

Don't thaw or heat frozen breast milk in a microwave or in boiling water. These can damage its nutritional and protective qualities and create hot spots that could scald your baby.

Thawed breast milk left at room temperature should be fed to your baby within 2 hours or thrown away. Never re-freeze breast milk once thawed.

Warming up milk

Healthy full-term babies can drink breast milk at room temperature or warmed to body temperature. Some have a preference, others don't seem to mind.

To warm your milk, place the breast milk bottle or bag into a cup, jug or bowl of lukewarm water for a few minutes to bring it to body temperature (37°C or 99°F). Alternatively, use a bottle warmer. Do not allow the temperature to go above 40°C (104°F).

Do not use a microwave, as this can overheat your milk.

Gently swirl the bottle or bag, without shaking or stirring, to mix any separated fat.

How partners can help when you are breastfeeding

All newborn babies need to feed frequently during the day and during the night. You can help your partner to breastfeed. Tips include:

- Praise your partner and tell her you love her.
- Give encouragement and listen to her.
- Ask her what she needs.
- Help her to position the baby near the breast to get ready for feeding – your midwife will support and guide you both.

- Ask family and friends to keep their visits short in the early days when you are both tired.
- Make healthy meals for your partner – feeding the mother is feeding the baby!
- Help out with housework.
- Plan something fun to do with any older children.

Bottle-feeding your baby

Feeding is not just about giving your baby food. It is also a time when you hold your baby close. This helps them feel special, safe and secure.

Your baby will love it when you look into their eyes. They will look back at you, delighted with the attention!

If you decide to bottle-feed your baby with expressed milk or formula, the tips below will help keep your baby safe and healthy. See page 153 (breast milk) and page 157 (formula) for advice on cleaning and sterilising feeding equipment.

Bottle-feeding tips

Before the feed

- Get everything you need ready before you start feeding.
- Make sure the milk is at the correct temperature. It should feel warm to the touch, not hot.
- Never heat your baby's milk in a microwave.

During the feed

- Make sure you and your baby are well supported and comfortable during feeds.
- Help your baby to avoid swallowing air while feeding – keep the teat full of milk.
- Wind your baby to help get rid of swallowed air if needed.

After the feed

At the end of the feed, sit and hold your baby upright – gently rub or pat their back for a while to bring up any wind.

Formula feeds

What is formula milk?

If you are thinking about using formula milk, talk to your midwife, postnatal ward nurse or public health nurse. They will talk to you about the:

- type of formula used for young babies
- cost
- safety of local water supply
- equipment needed
- risks of incorrect use of formula

Formula milk is also known as formula feed, baby formula or infant formula. Most formula milk is made from cows' milk.

It comes in powdered form or in 'ready to feed' cartons. Like any food, powdered infant formula is not sterile and may contain bacteria. This is why equipment like bottles and teats need to be sterilised (page 157).

Types of formula milk

First infant formula

First infant formula is the type of formula recommended for newborns. This should always be the formula you use and is recommended until your baby is 12 months old.

Hungry baby milk

Hungry baby formula contains more casein than whey. Casein is a protein that is harder for babies to digest.

It's often described as suitable for 'hungrier babies'. There is no evidence that hungry baby milk helps babies settle better.

Other types of milk

Do not give a baby under the age of 12 months:

- regular cow's milk
- sheep's milk
- goat's milk

- condensed milk
- plant-based milks like oat, almond or rice milk

Soy formula

Do not use soy formula unless it has been prescribed by your paediatrician or GP.

Water supply

Boiled tap water is usually the safest type of water to use. Know the safety of your local water supply (see epa.ie).

Bottled water

There may be times when you need to use bottled water, for example if travelling abroad. It is best not to use bottled water labelled as 'natural mineral water' to make up your baby's feeds as it can have high levels or sodium (salt) and other minerals. If this is the only water available, use it for the shortest time possible. It is important that your baby gets enough to drink.

Bottled water is not sterile. Always boil bottled water to make up formula. Use a kettle or saucepan to get a rolling boil for 1 minute. Cool in the normal way. Do not boil the same water again.

Automatic formula makers

The Food Safety Authority of Ireland (FSAI) does not recommend the use of formula preparation machines or automatic machines to prepare bottles of powdered infant formula. There is not enough research to support the safety of these machines.

What you need

To prepare formula milk correctly, you will need:

- a clean work surface
- facilities to wash your hands and equipment
- at least 6 bottles, lids and teats
- formula powder
- suitable water and a way to boil it
- a bottle brush and a small teat brush
- sterilising equipment like a steam, chemical or microwave kit
- tongs to help you grip the equipment

How to clean and sterilise equipment

You must sterilise all feeding equipment until your baby is at least 12 months old. This is the same if you are using expressed breast milk or formula.

Clean and sterilise all feeding equipment before you use it.

Cleaning

Follow these steps:

- Wash your hands well with soap and warm water.
- Dry your hands with a clean towel.
- Wash all the feeding equipment in hot soapy water, such as the bottles, teats, lids and tongs.
- Use a clean bottle brush and teat brush to scrub the inside and outside of the bottles and teats to make sure your remove any leftover milk from the hard-to-reach places.
- Rinse the bottles and teats well in clean running water.

You can use your dishwasher to clean bottles and feeding equipment that are dishwasher proof. Check with the manufacturer if you're not sure if the bottles or equipment can be used in a dishwasher. Dishwashers do not sterilise bottles or feeding equipment.

Sterilising

You can use boiling water, a chemical steriliser or a steam kit to sterilise equipment. A steam steriliser is the best. You can get plug-in or microwaveable sterilisers too.

If using boiling water

Fill a large saucepan with tap water and make sure all equipment is completely covered by the liquid. Make sure there are no trapped air bubbles. Cover the saucepan and bring it to the boil.

Boil for at least three minutes. Make sure the feeding equipment is fully covered with boiling water at all times. Keep the saucepan covered until you need to use the equipment.

Putting bottles together after sterilising

- Make sure your hands and the work surface are clean.
- Touching only the outside of the collar, place it over the teat and use sterile tongs to pull the teat through the collar.
- Screw the collar onto the bottle and tighten fully.
- Place the cap over the bottle, being sure not to touch the inside of the cap when doing this.
- Store the bottles in a clean place.
- If put together correctly the empty bottles and bottles with sterile water will be safe for 24 hours. If not used within 24 hours, sterilise again. Once you open a bottle to add water or powder it is not sterile.
- Keep all sterilising equipment and hot water out of reach of children.

Using formula milk safely

1. Empty your kettle and fill it with one litre (1l) of freshly drawn cold tap water and boil. Alternatively, boil one litre (1l) of water in a clean pan.
2. Leave the boiled water to cool in the kettle or pan. Cool it for 30 minutes, but no longer. This will make sure that the water is not too hot, but also that it is no less than 70°C.
3. Clean the work surface well. Wash your hands with soap and warm water and dry them on a clean towel.
4. Read the instructions on the formula's label carefully to find out how much water and powder you need.
5. Pour the correct amount of water into a sterilised bottle. Water that is 70°C is still hot enough to scald, so be careful.
6. Add the exact amount of formula to the boiled water using the clean scoop provided. Reseal the packaging to protect it from germs and moisture. Adding too much or too little formula could make your baby sick.
7. Screw the bottle lid tightly and shake well to mix the contents.
8. To cool the feed quickly, hold the bottle under cold running water or place it in a large bowl of cold water. Make sure that the cold water does not reach above the neck of the bottle.
9. To check the feed is not too hot, shake the bottle and place a drop of liquid on the inside of the wrist – it should feel lukewarm, not hot. Feed your baby.
10. Throw away any feed that your baby has not taken within 2 hours. If your baby is a slow feeder use a fresh feed after 2 hours.

Before you leave hospital, your nurse or midwife will explain how to safely prepare your baby's formula feed.

> For more information, see mychild.ie and safefood.eu

For breast-fed and formula fed babies

Vitamin D and your baby

Our bodies can make vitamin D from the sun. But babies cannot safely get the vitamin D they need from the sun.

Why your baby needs it

Your baby needs vitamin D to help them build strong bones, muscles and teeth. It also helps the immune system. Low levels of vitamin D in children can cause rickets. This is a condition that leads to soft bones.

Between 0 to 12 months babies grow very quickly and have a greater need for vitamin D to form strong bones.

Due to a change in EU law (February 2020) there is an increase in the amount of vitamin D3 added to infant formula. As a result, the Department of Health has changed its recommendation on vitamin D supplements.

All babies who are being breastfed should continue to get vitamin D3 supplement after birth, even if you took vitamin D3 during pregnancy or while breastfeeding.

You do not need to give your baby a vitamin D3 supplement if they are fed more than 300mls or 10 fluid oz (ounces) of infant formula a day.

Correct amount

You should give your baby 5 micrograms of vitamin D3 as a supplement every day from birth to 12 months if they are:

* breastfed
* taking less than 300mls or 10 fluid oz (ounces) of infant formula a day

Buying vitamin D3 supplements

There are many suitable infant vitamin D3 supplements available to buy in Ireland. Use a supplement that contains vitamin D only. Talk to your pharmacist and read the information on the label carefully.

Check the label on your vitamin D3 supplement for the number of drops or amount of liquid you need to give your baby.

You may need to give your baby the supplement in a different way with each new brand.

Bonding during feeds

Make the most of this time to bond with your baby:

* Stay in close contact – consider opening your shirt and doing skin-to-skin contact with your baby.
* Look into your baby's eyes and your baby will look back at you – this helps babies feel safe and loved.
* Take it slowly and enjoy the cuddles.
* Resist the urge to multi-task.
* Don't prop the bottle — this increases the risk of choking as well as potentially affecting bonding.

What is responsive feeding?

Responsive parenting is an important part of forming a healthy relationship with your baby. It means that you are responding sensitively to your baby while accepting their needs and signals.

This type of parenting helps your baby to form healthy brain connections and encourages feelings of safety and comfort. Your baby loves when you hold them close. It comforts your baby and helps them feel secure.

You can do responsive feeding by responding to your baby when they are showing signs of:

- hunger (early feeding cues) – see page 139
- distress

Tips for responsive breastfeeding
- Feed your baby whenever they show signs of wanting to breastfeed.
- Respond to your baby's early feeding cues.
- Do not try to time the feeds or feed to a schedule.
- Remember that you are not 'spoiling' your baby by responding to their needs in this way.

Tips for responsive bottle feeding
- Your baby will love it if you or your partner do most of the feeds – they know you best.
- Gently encourage the baby to root and invite them to take the teat.
- Pace the feed or go at your baby's pace – try not to rush.
- Never force your baby to take a full feed.

For partners

Here are some tips to help you bond with your baby, especially when they are being breastfed:

- Talk to them and sing to them.
- Cuddle, rock and lie with the baby on your bare chest – babies love skin-to-skin contact.
- Bathing, winding and nappy changing are all great ways to bond.

Common concerns when feeding

Contact your public health nurse (PHN) for support and advice on all aspects of feeding. Many health centres have regular well-baby clinics. These are run by public health nurses.

Colic

- Colic is excessive and frequent crying in a baby who appears to be otherwise healthy.
- It is not harmful. A baby with colic should still be thriving and gaining weight. Colic is a phase that lasts a few weeks.
- Talk to your GP or your public health nurse if you think your baby has colic.

Allergies

- Formula is based on cow's milk. Some babies can be allergic to a particular formula.
- Talk to your GP if you are worried. They can prescribe special formula feeds for your baby. Your GP may also refer your baby to a dietitian.
- Allergies are less common when breastfeeding but can happen.

Constipation

- Some babies may have one or more dirty nappies every day. Others may have one every few days.
- Constipation is when babies have difficulty pooing. The poos may be firm dry pellets which do not soak into the nappy.
- When a baby is straining, their face will often become red. They may grunt or make other noises. Straining can be normal. However, straining with crying is often a sign of constipation.
- Breastfed babies rarely become constipated. This is because breast milk contains a natural laxative.
- If your baby is constipated, give 30 ml of cooled boiled water one to two times per day. A bath and gently massaging your baby's tummy may help.
- Talk to your GP if your baby has not had a bowel motion after 2 to 3 days, or is very distressed.

Vomiting

- Small vomits are known as 'possets'. They are normal after a feed and common in young babies. Your baby will grow out of this. Some babies bring up more milk than others after a feed.
- It can be quite worrying when it happens. Make sure your baby is continuing to gain weight. Keep your baby upright (not lying down) for 20 minutes after a feed.
- If bottle-feeding, consider choosing a smaller teat. Your baby's gag reflex may be stimulated by milk flowing too fast.

If you feel something might be wrong

Trust your instincts. You know your baby better than anyone.

If you are worried about anything, contact your GP or public health nurse.

Contact your GP if:

- your baby is not thriving (losing weight or not gaining weight)
- the vomiting is forceful or projectile (sprays out of your baby's mouth for several feet)
- your baby seems to be in pain

Babies who need extra care

Some babies will need extra care after birth. They might need to stay in the postnatal ward, a special care baby unit (SCBU) or a neonatal intensive care unit (NICU). Sometimes this may mean your baby has to be transferred to another hospital.

This can be a very worrying and confusing time for parents. When your baby arrives too soon, you may feel unprepared. You may also have mixed feelings towards your baby. This is normal.

Reasons some babies need additional care:

- premature or low birth weight
- infection
- jaundice – a condition in newborns that causes the skin and the whites of the eyes to become yellow
- their mother had medical problems such as diabetes
- difficult birth
- they are waiting for surgery in a children's hospital

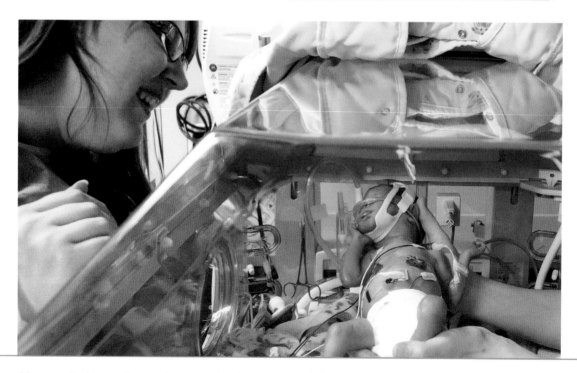

Physical contact with your baby

Babies who are very small usually need to be cared for in incubators. This helps them keep warm. They may be on a breathing machine. There may also be tubes and wires attached to your baby.

You can put your hands through the incubator's portholes and touch your baby. Always wash your hands before touching your baby. This is to prevent the spread of infections.

Your baby will benefit from hearing your voice and from contact with you. Once your baby is well enough, ask the staff to help you do skin-to-skin contact.

Feeding your premature or ill baby

When your baby is in special care, you may feel anxious and helpless. Breastfeeding is a very positive way you can help your baby's recovery. If your baby is too unwell to breastfeed, you can express your milk.

Colostrum

The milk you produce is tailor-made for your baby. It is full of antibodies to help them fight infection. The first milk you produce is called colostrum ('liquid gold'). Every drop is of benefit to your baby.

Hand expressing

The best way to collect your colostrum is by hand-expressing (see page 151). Your nurse or midwife will help you.

Your colostrum can be given to your baby through a special feeding tube. Once your baby is strong enough, you can breastfeed or bottle-feed expressed milk.

Understanding your baby's treatment

For a period of time, your baby's hospital ward becomes the centre of your universe. Talk to staff there, learn the routines and find out who will be caring for your baby.

Ask the nurse or midwife in the ward to:

- explain what everything is for
- show you how you can be involved in your baby's care

Your nurse or midwife is there to support and help you.

It is important you understand as much as possible about your baby's treatment. This means you can work with hospital staff to make sure your baby gets the best care. You may need to give your consent for some of the treatments your baby needs.

Comforting your baby

Some of the most important things you can do for your baby are:

- to comfort them
- make sure they are safe

Everything is new to your baby. They may easily feel startled, scared or upset. Your baby will feel reassured and loved if you comfort them. Simply being held close to you may calm them.

> You are not 'spoiling' your baby by picking them up when they cry. The more responsive you are to their cries in the early months, the less they cry when they're older. This is based on research.

Why is my baby crying?

Babies normally have at least one period of being unsettled each day. They cry for many reasons.

Crying is your baby's way of telling you that they need something.

Sometimes you need to think about all the possible reasons why your baby is crying to figure out what they need.

It can take time to learn what your baby is trying to communicate. Try to be patient with yourself as you get to know your baby.

Hungry or thirsty?

Your baby may be 'rooting' around for your breast. They may be making sucking motions with their mouth. These are early feeding cues and the best time to feed your baby.

What to try

Feed your baby.

Need a nappy change?

Some babies don't like feeling wet or dirty.

What to try

Check the nappy and change it if needed.

Wind?

'Wind' can happen when babies swallow. Air bubbles can become trapped in their tummy and cause a lot of discomfort. Some babies find it easy to burp. Others need your help.

Your baby will be unsettled if they have wind.

What to try

Hold your baby upright and gently rub or pat their back.

Tired, overtired or overstimulated?

Simple things like new faces and bright lights can be overwhelming for babies.

What to try

Take your baby to a darker room that is quiet and calm. Make soothing noises. You can also try soft music or white noise. White noise is a low frequency sound, for example from a vacuum cleaner. You can use the sound from white noise CDs, videos or apps.

Uncomfortable?

Babies don't like being cold. They like to feel cosy and warm. Be careful not to underdress or overdress your baby.

What to try

Check your baby is not too hot or cold. It is normal for a baby's hands and feet to feel cool but their tummy should be warm to touch.

Make sure there are no labels from clothing digging into their skin. Check there is no hair wrapped around their fingers or toes.

Need to be close to you?

Babies need to:

- be close to their parents
- hear their voices
- listen to their heartbeats

They also find movement soothing.

What to try

You can try:

- holding your baby close
- singing or talking to them
- carrying them with you
- placing them safely in a sling

Remember that you are not 'spoiling' your baby by responding to their cries.

None of the above?

Sometimes nothing you do seems to work.

What to try

Things you can try include:

- Go for a drive with your baby in their car seat.
- Take your baby on a walk in their buggy or pram.

- Leave their nappy off and let your baby kick their legs.
- Give them a bath.
- Ask your partner, family or friends for help.

Looking after yourself

Some babies cry more than others. Hearing your baby cry can be very upsetting.

It is normal to feel stressed when your baby is crying, especially if nothing you do seems to be helping.

This happens to almost all parents and to all babies. It is one of the hardest parts of being a parent. You are a caring parent. This will pass.

Once you know that your baby's needs are met, it is time to look after yourself.

Ways to care for yourself

- Ask for help. Someone you trust can take over while you get a break.
- Call a friend or family member for help, advice and support.
- Take deep breaths.
- Put on relaxing music to distract yourself.
- If you are worried about an underlying cause for the crying, contact your GP.

Contact your GP for any of the following reasons:

- the crying continues
- the crying sounds unusual
- you are worried your baby may be ill
- you are finding it hard to cope

Caring for your baby

No amount of planning and research fully prepares you for the reality of having a newborn baby.

The weight of a newborn baby is tiny compared to the weight of responsibility that you may feel.

It is common to feel like you don't have a clue what you are doing. Even doctors, nurses and midwives feel like this when they have their own babies!

Your public health nurse (PHN) is available to provide information and support on all aspects of caring for your baby. Your PHN will visit you at home within 72 hours of the birth. You will see them again as your baby grows (see page 199). Your PHN is usually based at your local HSE health centre.

Nappy changing tips

Whether you use disposable or cloth nappies, one thing is for sure. They all need to be changed!

1. Get everything ready before you begin.
2. If you are using a changing table, make sure everything you need is within reach.
3. Wash your hands before removing the nappy.
4. Clean your baby's genitals and bottom with cotton wool and water or an unscented wipe.
5. Gently lift your baby's legs by holding their ankles. This allows you to clean underneath.
6. For girls and boys, always wipe from front to back.
7. For a baby boy, there is no need to retract the foreskin. Point his penis downwards before replacing the nappy.
8. Let the area dry. There is no need to use powders.
9. Slide a new and open nappy under your baby by gently lifting their legs at the ankles. The new nappy should be snug but not tight.
10. Wash your hands after changing the nappy.

Safe nappy changing

Risk of falling

Never leave your baby alone on a raised surface, even for a few seconds. Babies can roll off changing tables, beds and other raised surfaces. These falls can result in serious head injuries.

Risk of suffocation from nappy bags or sacks

Nappy disposal bags and sacks and other plastic bags are a suffocation risk.

Do not store nappy sacks or any other plastic material within your baby's reach.

Building a bond

Nappy changes are another chance to build a bond with your baby. You can make this time special by:

- talking to your baby
- explaining to them what you are doing
- singing and playing with them

Nappy rash

Nappy rash is a red, moist or broken area on your baby's bottom.

Most babies get nappy rash at some time. Some babies are more sensitive than others.

Your baby's skin needs to be clean and dry to help prevent nappy rash.

If your baby's bottom has redness or spots:

- change their nappy more often
- give them time without a nappy
- gently clean your baby's bum from front to back
- apply a small amount of barrier cream to protect your baby's skin – ask your pharmacist or public health nurse for advice on creams and powders for treating nappy rash
- contact your GP if the rash seems painful and does not go away

Your baby's nappies

Most babies have:

- at least 6 wet nappies each day
- at least 1 dirty nappy each day – some breastfed babies may have more or less than this

If the bowel motion (poo) passed looks soft, your baby is not constipated.

"Your touch is so important to me. It helps my body and brain develop in so many ways."

Caring for the umbilical cord

After the birth, your midwife, obstetrician or partner will cut the umbilical cord. This will leave a stump on your baby's tummy where the umbilical cord is cut. You need to keep this area clean and dry while waiting for the stump to fall off.

Your baby's umbilical cord stump will fall off in its own time, usually 5 to 15 days after birth.

Before the umbilical cord stump falls off:

- check the umbilical cord at every nappy change to make sure there is no redness there
- wash your hands before and after you touch the cord
- clean around the base of the cord if needed with cotton wool and cooled boiled water
- keep the belly button area dry after you clean it
- fold your baby's nappy down, away from the stump
- make sure that the nappy is not covering the cord

After the stump falls off

The umbilical stump will dry out, turn black and drop off. After the stump comes off, it usually takes about seven to 10 days for the belly button to heal completely.

Ask your midwife or public health nurse for advice if you see any bleeding or discharge from your baby's belly button.

Go to your GP if you see redness on the skin of your baby's stomach around the stump of the cord, or there is a foul smell.

Bathing your baby

Your midwife or public health nurse will show you how to bathe your baby for the first time. Don't be afraid to ask for help or to see it done once or twice before you try.

How often

You don't need to bathe your baby every day, although you can if it relaxes and soothes them. Two or three baths a week is enough to keep your baby clean.

You can also give your baby a 'top and tail' clean instead of a bath. When you are more confident, you can wash your baby in the main bath or in the sink, or in their own small baby bath.

'Top and tail' wash

Use pieces of cotton wool and a bowl of warm water. Wet each piece of cotton wool in the bowl and then squeeze it out so it is just damp when you use it.

Use separate pieces of the cotton wool to clean:

- your baby's face and hands
- the folds or creases under the neck
- the folds and creases under arms
- the nappy area

"Bath time can be 'bond time'! Talk to me as you wash me. I love hearing your voice, it helps me relax."

When to do it

Choose a time when they are not too hungry or tired. It's best not to bathe them just after a feed.

What you need

Make sure the room you are bathing them in is warm.

Have everything you need ready before you start:

- a baby bath or basin
- a clean nappy
- clean clothes
- two towels
- some cotton wool.

Use plain water and no liquid soaps for babies under 1 month.

Getting the water ready

Put the cold water in the basin or bath first. Then put the warm water in. If your bath has a single tap with a hot and cold feed, make sure you run the cold water again to cool the taps so they won't burn your baby.

Fill the basin, bath, baby bath or sink until it has 8cm to 10cm or so of water in it.

The temperature should be about 36°C. You can use a bath thermometer to test this.

Always check the temperature of the bathwater with your elbow. Your hands are not heat-sensitive enough. Mix the water well to ensure there are no 'hot spots'.

Your baby's skin needs cooler water than your own. Water that may not feel hot to you could be too hot for your baby.

How to bathe your baby

1. Hold your baby on your knee and clean their face.
2. Hold their head over the basin and wash their hair.
3. Make sure their head is dried.
4. Slip off the nappy and wipe their bottom.
5. Get ready to lower your baby into the basin. Have one of your arms behind their shoulders and neck, holding their outside arm with your hand.
6. Place your other hand under their bottom.
7. Lower your baby slowly into the water so they don't feel as though they are falling.
8. When their bottom is resting on the floor of the basin or bath, you can remove that hand to wash them.
9. Use your other hand to keep your baby's head out of the water.
10. When finished, put the hand you used to wash them back under their bottom.
11. Hold their legs with that arm as they will be slippery. Then lift them out onto the towel.
12. Lift baby out and pat them dry, don't forget to dry their skin folds and creases.
13. Empty the basin, bath, baby bath or sink.

Now is a good time to try baby massage, this can help soothe them. Don't use any oils on their skin for the first month.

Bath safety

Babies under 12 months are at greatest risk of drowning in the bath. Drowning can happen in silence, in an instant and in a very small amount of water.

Never leave your baby alone in the bath, not even for a second.

Your baby's fingernails

Your baby's nails are very soft in the first few weeks after birth. You could easily cut baby's skin when you cut the nails. You may find it better to gently peel the nails off or use an emery board to file the nails.

After a week or two, buy special baby nail clippers or small round-ended safety nail scissors from a pharmacy. Wait until baby is relaxed or asleep before trying to cut nails. Ask someone else to help you if you need to.

Cold sores? Keep your baby safe from infection

If you develop a cold sore or think you're coming down with a herpes infection, take these precautions:

- do not kiss your baby
- wash your hands before contact with your baby
- wash your hands before breastfeeding and cover up any cold sores to avoid accidentally touching your mouth and then breast – this is enough to transfer the virus

Make sure other people including visitors take the same precautions if they have a cold sore or think they may be about to get one.

Playing with your baby

"Hold a toy over my pram or cot to help me learn."

"Smile at me and hold me close. This helps me feel safe."

"Cuddle me, touch me, talk to me, sing to me. I will get excited when I hear or see you. I will cuddle into you."

"When you are close by, I feel I can safely explore my world."

"I love it when you talk to me. When I say "aah" and you say "ooh" - that's a conversation!"

Playing with your baby makes your bond stronger. It helps them to learn and develop. Even newborn babies learn from their parents. Soon they will respond to your touch and the tone of your voice.

Tummy time

Your baby should always be placed on their back to sleep. This helps to reduce the risk of sudden infant death syndrome (cot death).

When your baby is awake, it is important that they spend time on their tummy. This helps their development. Tummy time from birth helps develop better head control and stronger muscles.

Here are some ways to put tummy time into your baby's routine:

Tummy-to-tummy

Lie down on the floor or a bed. You can lie flat or prop yourself up on pillows. Place your baby on your chest or tummy so that you're face-to-face. Always hold your baby firmly for safety.

Eye-level smile

Get down level with your baby to encourage eye contact.

Roll up a blanket and place it under their chest and upper arms for added support.

Lap soothe

Place your baby face-down across your lap to burp or soothe them.

A hand on your baby's bottom will help them feel steady and calm.

Tummy-down carry

Carry your baby 'tummy down'. To do this, slide one hand under the tummy and between the legs. Nestle your baby close to your body.

Tummy minute

Place your baby on their tummy for one or two minutes every time you change them.

Information and images reproduced from pathways.org.

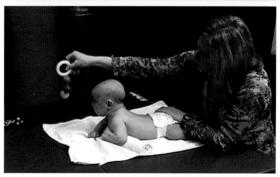

Your baby's first health checks

Midwife examinations

Your midwife will examine your baby each day during your hospital stay. If you have a home birth, your midwife will do this at your home.

They will ask about your baby's feeding patterns and wet and dirty nappies. They will check your baby for jaundice and will look at the umbilical cord area.

Your midwife, nurse on the postnatal ward or care assistant will give you advice on caring for your baby. This includes bathing and nappy changing. Your midwife will also help you start breastfeeding.

Jaundice

Jaundice causes skin and eyes to have a yellow colour. It is a common and usually harmless condition in newborns. A baby with jaundice may be sleepy. Your midwife will encourage you to wake the baby for feeds.

If your midwife is concerned about your baby's jaundice, they may perform a test called a 'bilimeter'. This is a small device that is placed on your baby's forehead. If this gives a high reading, a paediatric doctor will be called. They may take a sample of blood from your baby.

If your baby needs treatment, the most common treatment is 'phototherapy'. This means your baby is placed under bright lights for a period of time.

Full newborn clinical examination

All babies will have a thorough physical examination. This is done by a paediatric doctor or a specialist midwife before you both go home from hospital. Babies born at home will be examined by a specialist midwife or your GP.

The doctor or midwife examines your baby from head to toe. This will not hurt your baby although it is normal for babies to cry when they're being examined.

This examination is done to check your baby's general health. It is also done to see (screen) if your baby might have certain conditions of their eyes, heart, hips and testes. The examination is done to spot any problems as early as possible so treatment can be started.

However, sometimes screening does not identify all babies who are at risk. So if you have any concerns about your baby, talk to your GP or public health nurse.

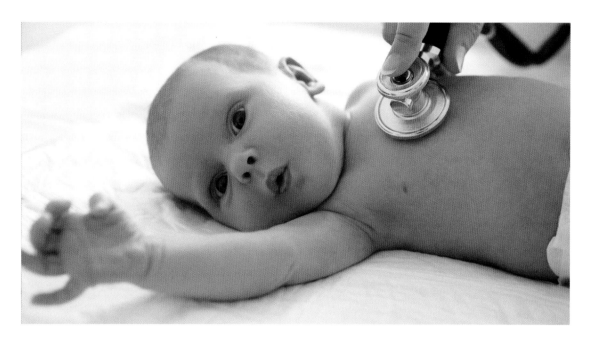

Your baby's eyes

The doctor or midwife will shine a light into your baby's eyes. This is to detect cataracts. Cataracts are a clouding of the lense of the eye. Your baby might need surgery if they have a cataract.

Your baby's heart

A probe will be placed on your baby's foot to check oxygen levels. The doctor or midwife will listen to your baby's heart with a stethoscope. They will check your baby's pulses.

If the results of this examination are not normal, your baby might need extra tests. These might include a tracing of their heart (ECG) or a scan of their heart (echocardiogram).

Your baby's hips

The doctor or midwife will gently bend your baby's leg upwards and rotate their hips outwards.

This test checks for dislocated hips. If this examination is not normal, your baby's hips will be checked in a few weeks using an ultrasound scan.

Your baby's testes

This examination is done on boys. It is to check that the testicles are in the right place.

The testicles are normally in the right place by six months. If they're not, your baby may need surgery.

Hearing test (newborn hearing screening)

Every baby is offered a newborn hearing screening test. For babies born in a hospital, this is done before leaving. The test is done by a trained hearing screener.

One to two babies in every 1,000 are born with a hearing problem. This can be hard to detect.

Testing your baby's hearing means that any problems can be detected early. Every baby should have this test even if there is no family history of hearing loss.

What does the test involve?

A soft earpiece is placed in your baby's ear. Clicking sounds are sent down the ear. These sounds usually cause an echo in your baby's inner ear. The equipment detects this echo.

Will the test hurt my baby?

This test does not hurt. You can stay with your baby while it is being done.

When will I get the results?

You will get the results immediately.

What if the test detects a problem?

A second hearing test will be done while your baby is sleeping.

Heel prick (newborn bloodspot screening)

Your baby will be offered newborn bloodspot screening in the first week after birth. This is also known as the 'heel prick'.

This is to see if they are at risk of having some rare but serious conditions.

What does it involve?

The midwife or public health nurse will gently prick the heel of your baby's foot. This is to collect some drops of blood onto a special card.

Will it hurt my baby?

Your baby may feel a little discomfort. You can help by:

- making sure your baby is warm and comfortable
- being ready to feed and cuddle your baby afterwards

When will I get the results?

You will be contacted if your baby is at risk of having one of the conditions. A repeat may be needed if the results are unclear.

What if it detects a problem?

If your baby is at risk of having one of these conditions, you will be referred to a healthcare team. Most babies grow healthy and well once treatment is started early.

What your baby needs

"One of the most important gifts you can give me is something money cannot buy. That is my relationship with you."

If babies could talk, they would probably tell us that they have very simple needs.

They need to be:

- loved
- fed
- warm and safe
- close to their parents

There are so many items out there for new babies. It can be confusing to know just what your baby needs. When you come home with your newborn, you won't need too much.

When buying products

Follow the manufacturer's instructions. Always assemble, install and use correctly.

Make sure that any equipment, toys and clothing you buy:

- is in perfect condition
- meets EU safety standards

Something to wear

Babies grow very quickly. In the first few weeks, you only need a small amount of clothes. Go for comfortable, soft and easy to wash clothes.

You'll need:

- baby grows (all-in-ones)
- vests
- cardigans
- a warm hat, coat or all in one suit
- socks
- mittens for colder weather
- a sunhat in summer

If something gets caught around your baby's neck, this could strangle them. Never put items on any part of your baby's body that could strangle them. These include necklaces, clothes or hats with strings attached, hairbands and belts.

Do not use amber teething jewellery

Do not put amber teething necklaces, bracelets and anklets on your baby. They could choke on them.

Somewhere to sleep

Your baby should sleep in a Moses basket or cot with a mattress that meets safety standards.

You'll need:

- a Moses basket or cot
- a mattress
- sheets
- cellular blankets (these have 'holes' in them allowing air to circulate and can help prevent your baby overheating)

If you are borrowing or buying a second-hand cot or Moses basket, buy a new mattress. The mattress should be firm and flat. It should fit the cot correctly and have a removable, washable cover.

> Pillows, cushion, sleep positioners and other similar products are not recommended. They are a suffocation risk.

Something to take them out and about

You'll need:

- a car seat
- a way to carry them when you're out and about - this could be a pram, pushchair, buggy, stroller, sling or baby carrier

Car-seats must be safe and suitable to your baby's height and weight. See page 180.

Pushchairs and strollers are only suitable for newborns if they recline fully.

Most baby carriers or slings are attached by straps and your baby is carried in front of you. Many babies like this because of the sensation of being close to you and warm. Make sure you use them correctly for your baby's safety.

5-point safety harness

Make sure all sitting devices like strollers, pushchairs, high chairs and car seats have a 5-point safety harness.

Something for nappy changes

You will need:

- nappies
- cotton wool or fragrance-free and alcohol-free wipes

- nappy bin or paper nappy bags – plastic nappy sacks and bags are a suffocation risk
- lotions – read the label to make sure they are hypoallergenic, dye-free and fragrance-free
- antibacterial hand wash so you can wash your hands before and after changing a nappy

Changing bag

A changing bag is useful for holding the nappies, wipes and anything else you need when not at home. Changing bags generally come with small reusable changing mats. If not, you might like to bring a changing mat or a towel.

Some feeding equipment

You will need plenty of muslin cloths and bibs.

Bibs can be a suffocation risk. Always remove your baby's bib after feeding.

Do not put them to sleep wearing a bib.

Breastfeeding

If you are breastfeeding, you will need very little equipment. You may want to make sure you have:

- nursing bras
- breast pads
- nipple cream such as lanolin

As your baby grows, you may want to express milk when you are going to be away from them. It may be worthwhile investing in a breast pump. You will also need sterilising equipment and bottles if you are expressing milk.

Formula feeding

If you are formula feeding, see page 157.

Something to keep them clean

You'll need:

- a bath or basin
- towels - baby bath towels are useful but not essential. Small bath towels are just as good

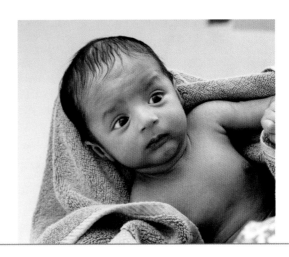

Car seats

Rearward-facing

Your baby's first car seat should be rearward-facing. This is the safest position for them to be in. This means the car seat is facing the back of the car. Check it is suitable for newborns. Never put a rearward-facing car seat in the front passenger seat if there is an active front passenger airbag. This is illegal and very dangerous.

Second-hand

Avoid buying a second-hand car seat, unless you are sure of its safety history. If the car seat was in a vehicle during a crash, it may have damage you can't see.

Your baby's car seat needs to be fitted correctly to keep them safe. Choose a retailer who can:

- advise you on which type of car seat is suitable for your child's height and weight
- expertly fit the car seat into your car to make sure it is a suitable match
- show you how the child seat should be fitted into your car

The Road Safety Authority (RSA) has a free 'check it fits' service. See rsa.ie

---

How to know if the harness is tight enough

The harness or straps of your baby's car seat are safest when they are snug.

In a rearward-facing car seat:

- Only two fingers should be able to fit between the top of your baby's shoulders and the harness.
- Your fingers should be unable to rotate (turn) in that position.

Blankets

Use blankets rather than bulky jackets to keep your baby warm in cooler weather.

Keeping your baby safe on journeys

Sleeping in a sitting position can cause your baby's head to flop forward. This can make it difficult to breathe.

Regular breaks

Do not leave your baby in a car seat for a long period. Take regular breaks (at least every 2 hours) on long journeys. Remove your baby from their car seat and allow them to lie flat on your lap.

Once you have reached your destination, remove your baby from the car seat.

Premature and low birth weight babies

If your baby is premature or low birth weight, talk to medical staff in the hospital. Ask them if it is safe for your baby to travel in a car seat.

Sleep

Some babies sleep more than others. Some sleep for long periods, others for short bursts. Some sleep through the night. Your baby is unique, and may sleep differently to other babies. A baby's sleep pattern is probably not going to fit in with your sleep pattern. Try to sleep when the baby sleeps.

Coping with disturbed sleep

Newborn babies will wake up to be fed. This can be very hard to cope with. Remember, this will pass.

It doesn't matter which feeding method you use. Newborn babies will wake regardless. Do not listen to people who tell you otherwise.

Your body needs rest. If you have a partner, ask them to help. Get help with cooking and chores so you can grab a nap.

Tips to help your baby be a 'good sleeper'

Responsive parenting is about responding to your baby's needs. It is an important part of 'attachment' or bonding with your baby.

Newborn babies are too young to follow strict routines. You can use responsive parenting tips to help your baby become a 'good sleeper'. It is never too early to start.

- Play with your baby when they are awake during the day.
- Have a relaxing bedtime routine like a bath and massage – your baby will soon link these activities with sleep.
- Put your baby to bed drowsy but awake.
- Give your baby time to settle down – they may fuss or cry before falling asleep.
- Expect frequent stirring at night – wait a few minutes to see if your baby falls back to sleep by themselves.
- Use a soft voice, gentle movements and dim lights with your baby if they wake during the night.
- Respect your baby's preferences – they may be a night owl or an early bird.

"It is not possible to 'spoil' me. When I know I can count on you, it helps me learn the skills I need to soothe myself."

Reducing the risk of cot death

Cot death is also called sudden infant death syndrome (SIDS). It is the sudden and unexpected death while sleeping of a baby who seems healthy. Cot death is rare. The cause is not known.

But research has shown that you can take steps to significantly reduce the risk. It is important to take precautions, while not letting fear spoil precious times with your baby. Share the tips on reducing cot death risk with everyone who looks after your baby.

You may be given more advice from your paediatrician, neonatologist, neonatal intensive care nurse, special care baby unit nurse, midwife, GP or public health nurse if your baby has specific health needs.

Safe sleep position

Back to sleep

Always place your baby on their back to sleep. Putting your baby to sleep on their back does not increase the risk of choking if they vomit.

Babies who sleep on their tummies have a higher risk of cot death. It is not safe to place your baby on their side to sleep because they may roll onto their tummy.

Head position

If your baby always lies with their head in the same position they might develop a 'flat head'. This is called plagiocephaly.

You can prevent this when putting your baby down to sleep on their back. When they are lying flat, you can alternate position their head so that sometimes they face left and sometimes they face right.

Keep the head and face uncovered

Keep your baby's face and head uncovered while asleep. Tuck blankets in loosely but securely, no higher than your baby's shoulders.

Feet towards the foot of the cot

Place your baby with their feet pointing to the foot of the cot, crib, Moses basket or pram. This means they can't wriggle down under the covers.

Where your baby should sleep

The safest place for your baby to sleep is in a cot in your bedroom. Their risk of cot death is lower there than for babies who sleep in a separate room. Keep your baby's cot in your room for at least the first 6 months.

Bed sharing or co-sleeping in the same bed can be dangerous. It can increase your baby's risk of suffocation and overheating.

Do not share a bed with your baby if you or your partner:

- are smokers
- have taken alcohol, drugs (legal or illegal) or medication that may make you drowsy
- are over tired

Bed-sharing is not recommended if your baby:

- is less than 3 months old
- was premature (born before 37 weeks)
- had a low birth weight – less than 2.5kg (kilograms) or 5.5lbs (pounds)

If you are under the influence of alcohol or drugs, get someone else to care for your baby until you are sober.

Make sure the cot is in good condition and properly assembled. The mattress should be clean, firm and flat with no tears. It must fit the cot correctly.

Keep it clear

Do not have any soft objects and anything loose or fluffy in your baby's cot. These could suffocate or smother your baby. This includes pillows, toys, cushions, sleep positioners and other similar products.

Sitting and carrying devices

Cot death does not only happen in a cot. It may happen in a pram, bed, car seat, baby seat or anywhere a baby is sleeping.

Sleeping in a sitting position can make it difficult for your baby to breathe. Never leave your baby unsupervised in a sitting device. This includes a car seat, baby seat, sling, carrier or similar products. These sitting and carrying devices are not recommended for routine sleep in the home.

If your baby falls asleep in a sitting position, they should be placed on their back to sleep as soon as possible.

Sofa, armchairs and furniture

Never fall asleep while holding your baby on a sofa, couch, armchair or beanbag.

Sleep temperature

Overheating can increase your baby's risk of cot death. A baby can overheat when asleep because of too much bedding or clothes, or because the room is too hot.

Room temperature

The room where your baby is sleeping should be between 16°C to 20°C. You can use a room thermometer to check the temperature. Never place your baby to sleep next to a radiator, heater, fire or in direct sunlight.

Blankets

Cotton cellular blankets are best. The tiny holes allow air to circulate.

Checking your baby

To check how warm your baby is, look for sweating or feel their tummy. Their tummy should feel warm but not too hot. Other signs of being too warm include flushed or red cheeks.

It is normal for a baby's hands and feet to feel cool.

No hats while sleeping

Babies lose heat through their heads. Your baby could overheat if they wear a hat while sleeping.

Do not let your baby go to sleep wearing a hat, unless advised to do so by your doctor or midwife.

Hats are used immediately after birth to keep a baby's temperature stable. They are not needed for sleep after then.

Smoke-free

Create a smoke-free zone for your baby. Do not smoke during pregnancy and don't let anyone smoke in your home, car or around your baby.

Breastfeeding

Breastfeed your baby, if possible. If feeding in bed, always put your baby back into their own cot.

Soothers and dodies

Some research suggests using a soother (dummy) at the start of sleep may reduce the risk of cot death.

If you choose to give your baby a soother:

- Offer the soother to your baby every time they are going to sleep.
- Do not force your baby to use a soother if your baby does not like it.
- Do not worry if the soother falls out while your baby is asleep.
- If you're breastfeeding, wait until this is well-established before introducing a soother.
- Do not use clips or chains to attach soother to your baby's clothes as this is a choking risk.

If you're worried

Get medical advice early and quickly if your baby seems unwell.
Call 999 or 112 if it's an emergency.

For more information on cot death, contact the National Paediatric Mortality
Register. Phone 01 878 8455 or email npmr@cuh.ie

 Child safety

Unintentional injuries (accidents) are the leading cause of death in children who don't have underlying medical problems. Most childhood injuries are predictable and preventable. The best way to keep your baby safe is to stay close to them.

Children have fearless curiosity. They can rapidly develop new skills. This can cause them to get into dangerous situations. Make sure your baby's environment is safe at all times.

Your public health nurse will provide child safety information as part of your baby's child health assessments.

"I'm depending on you to keep me safe. Please watch me at all times."

Be prepared for emergencies

In an emergency it can be difficult to think clearly. Take the thinking out of it by being prepared.

Store emergency numbers on your phone:

- 999 or 112 for ambulance, fire brigade, Garda Síochána and Irish Coast Guard
- your GP
- your local GP Out of Hours service
- your local children's hospital
- National Poisons Information Centre on 01 809 2166 (8am to 10pm, 7 days a week)

Eircode

Learn your Eircode – this can help an ambulance find your home more quickly.

Can you give good directions to your home? If not, write them out and leave them somewhere they will be seen.

First aid

Have a first aid kit in your home. Consider doing a first aid course. The Irish Red Cross has an app with easy-to-follow tips for over 20 common first aid scenarios. See the app store or redcross.ie

Child-proofing your home

Being able to explore their environment is important for your baby's development. Childproofing your home keeps little explorers safe as they grow and learn about the world around them.

This means spotting potential dangers and then taking action to sort them. Childproofing can be done gradually. As your baby grows and becomes more mobile, you need to anticipate dangers and 'childproof' your home more regularly.

Anticipation
Thinking 'safety

+

Action
Acting 'safely'

=

Injury prevention
In 90% of cases

Did you know?

Most injuries among children aged 0 to 5 happen in the home. Supervising your baby at all times is the most effective way to keep them safe.

Family and friends may want to buy something for your baby. They might ask you: "Is there something in particular you need?"

You could suggest equipment that will keep your baby safe now or when they are older, such as a baby thermometer.

Equipment at home

All the equipment your baby uses should:

- meet current safety standards
- be in perfect condition
- be assembled, installed and used correctly – follow manufacturer's instructions

Examples of equipment that help keep your baby safe at home:

- smoke alarms
- carbon monoxide alarms in every room where you burn fuel
- fire blanket and fire extinguisher – store between the cooker and room exit
- sparkguard – use on open fires
- fireguard for open fires and stoves – secure to wall and use with a sparkguard
- thermometers for room temperature, bath water and your baby's temperature

Working smoke alarms

A smoke alarm on each floor in your home is a minimum. Aim to have one in every room so that a fire will be discovered as early as possible. Test regularly (once a week is recommended).

Equipment for out and about

Prams, pushchairs, strollers or buggies

Your pram, pushchair, stroller or buggy should:

- be sturdy
- have brakes that work
- comply with current European safety regulations

Supervise your baby at all times – toddlers and pets can knock over strollers.

Five-point harness and straps

Make sure your baby's sitting devices like car seats and strollers have a five-point harness — that's a harness with five straps that are all properly secured to provide really effective restraint.

Baby carriers and slings

Always follow **TICKS** guidelines:

- **T**ight
- **I**n view at all times
- **C**lose enough to kiss
- **K**eep chin off chest
- **S**upported back

Baby carriers and slings can be a suffocation risk to your baby unless you use them correctly.

Putting your baby into a carrier or sling

Put your baby in clothes that won't make them too warm. Be careful when you put your baby into or remove them from a sling. Ask for help if you need it.

Always follow the TICKS guidelines (see picture). Make sure:

- your baby's chin is not pressed into their chest
- their face is not pressed into the fabric of the sling or your clothing
- their legs are not bunched against their stomach
- you can see your baby's face
- you check your baby often

Never leave your baby alone in a carrier or sling.

Slings may not suit some babies

Contact your GP or paediatrician before using a sling, baby carrier or baby-wearing coat if your baby is younger than four months, was premature, born with low birth weight or has a medical condition, including respiratory conditions and colds.

When carrying your baby

Do not use a carrier or sling if you are doing things that could lead to an injury. This includes cooking, running, cycling or having hot drinks like tea and coffee.

Wear and tear

Check your carrier for wear and tear before every use. Look for ripped seams, torn straps and damaged hardware. If your sling has rings, make sure the fabric cannot slip.

Protecting your newborn during everyday activities

Holding your baby

Your baby's head is big and heavy, compared to the size of their neck and body. Always support your baby's head.

Hold your baby during feeds. If using a bottle, always hold it yourself. Never prop it onto something else.

High surfaces

When your baby is on a high surface like a table, always keep one hand on them. Never leave your child unattended, not even for a second.

Look out for choking and strangulation risks

Keep small objects out of reach. Check for strangulation risks, such as blind cords and strings on clothes.

Preventing burns and scalds

Do not hold your baby when you are cooking or drinking hot drinks.

When getting ready to bathe your baby, put the cold water into the basin or bath first. Always check the temperature of the water before placing your baby in. See page 170.

Share child safety information with everyone who takes care of your child.

Safety around pets

Our four-legged friends are like part of the family. But there are things to keep in mind when bringing your baby home if you have pets.

- No pet is 100% safe around children.
- Introduce your baby slowly to your pet.
- Never leave your baby alone with a dog, cat or any pet. The rule is the same when your baby is awake or sleeping.
- Pets can carry infections, so wash your baby's hands if they touch your pet or their toys, bed, litter or cage.
- Keep sick animals away from your baby.
- Wash your hands carefully after handling your pet, its litter tray, droppings, feed bowls, bedding, toys or cage.

Go to your GP, out of hours GP or nearest hospital emergency department if your baby is bitten or scratched by a pet.

Some types of pets may be unsuitable when you have a baby:

Reptiles and turtles

Reptiles such as snakes, turtles, tortoises and lizards are not suitable for homes with children under age 5. They carry a range of germs that could make your baby very ill or even cause death.

Dogs with behavioural problems

Any dog with behavioural problems requires an additional level of care, control and supervision.

Vaccines

Immunising or vaccinating your baby may save their life. Vaccines protect them from some serious or even fatal diseases. Information about immunisations is available from your GP, practice nurse or public health nurse.

No parent likes the idea of their baby being given an injection. But remember:

- Vaccinations are quick, safe and effective.
- Vaccinating your baby protects them from diseases so they can fight them more easily.
- If you don't vaccinate your child, there is a chance they could become very ill or even die from disease.
- Be ready with a feed or a hug for your baby and the vaccination will be forgotten in seconds.

Remember it takes 5 visits to your GP or GP practice nurse to fully vaccinate your baby.

See immunisation.ie for more information on your child's vaccines, including the BCG vaccine.

Diseases your baby will be protected against

Primary **Childhood** Immunisation Schedule

Children born on or after 1 October 2016

Age		Vaccination
2 months	**Visit 1**	**6 in 1+PCV+MenB+Rotavirus** **3 Injections+Oral Drops**
4 months	**Visit 2**	6 in 1+MenB+Rotavirus 2 Injections+Oral Drops
6 months	**Visit 3**	6 in 1+PCV+MenC 3 Injections

No Rotavirus vaccine on or after 8 months 0 days

Age		Vaccination
12 months	**Visit 4**	**MMR+MenB** **2 Injections**
13 months	**Visit 5**	Hib/MenC+PCV 2 Injections

Remember to give your baby 3 doses of liquid infant paracetamol after the 2 and 4 month MenB vaccines.

1. Give 2.5 mls (60 mg) of liquid infant paracetamol at the time of the immunisation or shortly after.
2. Give a second dose of 2.5 mls (60 mg) 4 to 6 hours after the first dose.
3. Give a third dose of 2.5 mls (60 mg) 4 to 6 hours after the second dose.

Remember five visits to your GP (doctor)

www.immunisation.ie

Order code: HNI00984

Feidhmeannacht na Seirbhíse Sláinte
Health Service Executive

Bonding with your baby

Most babies are born ready to connect with you. They have instinctive behaviours.

These include:

- crying
- clinging to you
- sucking
- reaching
- smiling and gurgling later on

These behaviours are designed to keep you close. Through these behaviours, the first bonds of attachment develop.

Attachment

Attachment is a word to describe a relationship. This begins with the normal everyday interactions between a parent and a baby.

You are so busy feeding your baby, comforting them and keeping them warm and safe. During all of this, your little baby is learning from you.

Learning about the world

Your baby is learning about you from your touch, your voice and your smell. Through you, they are learning about the world.

Your baby is developing a healthy and secure attachment to you. This is very important for their mental wellbeing. Scientists are proving that babies who bond with their parent are less likely to have social, emotional and behavioural problems later in life.

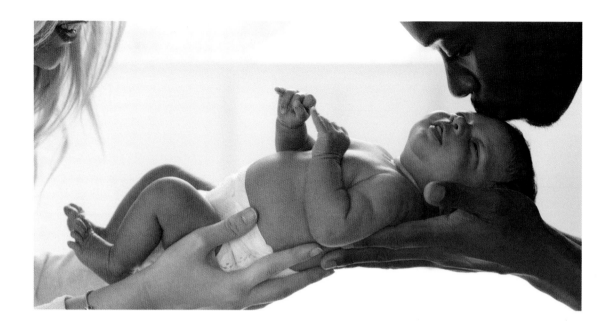

How to help form a strong attachment (bond)

- Comfort your baby when they need it.
- Keep them safe, warm and fed.
- Breastfeed if you can, as this can help with attachment.
- Respond to your baby's cues such as smiling, cooing and crying.
- Talk and sing to your baby.
- If you or your family speak another language, use this often to speak to your baby.
- Reduce your own screen time (TVs, computers, phones) when you are with your baby.

The father or partner's role

- Lie down with your newborn on your chest. (Never fall asleep like this).
- Consider taking paternity leave to spend more time with your baby.
- Talk and sing to your baby.
- If your baby is being breastfed, find other ways to spend good quality time with them. See page 154.
- Watch the mother for signs of exhaustion or depression. Listen to them and give support and encouragement.

Registering your baby's birth

It is the law in Ireland that you must register a birth. You will need your baby's birth certificate for many things. For example, to apply for a passport or child benefit allowance.

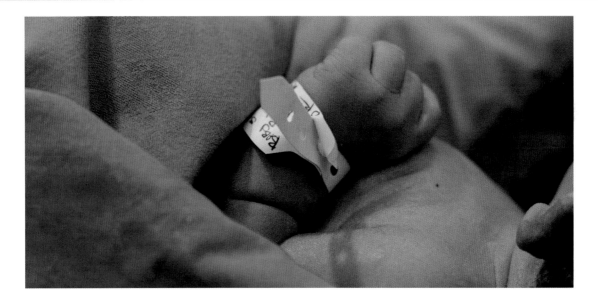

If your baby is born in a hospital, staff will send a birth registration form to the civil registration service. Your community midwife will arrange this if your baby is born at home.

You will then need to register the birth yourself. You have to do this before your baby is three months old.

Where to do it

You can do this at any civil registration office, no matter where in the Republic of Ireland your baby was born.

A qualified informant must register the birth. A qualified informant is usually a parent or both parents.

For more information, including what you need to bring with you, search for 'register a birth' on HSE.ie

Registering a birth is free. There is a fee to get a birth certificate.

How a baby affects your relationship

The transition from being a couple to becoming a family of three or more can have an effect on your relationship.
In many ways, your relationship may be stronger than ever. You will experience the joys and challenges of parenting together. You may view your partner in a new light as you watch them adjusting to their new role as a parent.

Lack of sleep

Occasionally there can be tension and issues in a relationship after the birth of a baby. A big factor in this is tiredness and lack of sleep.

Working together to try and make sure everyone gets as much sleep as possible will help. This may mean a temporary change in sleeping arrangements. For example, one parent might get a few hours' sleep in a different room.

Time together

The busy days (and nights!) with a newborn baby can mean that it is difficult to find time together as a couple.

It is common to not feel like having sex for a while after a baby is born.

This could be because of:

- the need for physical and emotional recovery from childbirth
- feeling tired

Occasionally you may find that you have differing views on various aspects of parenting.

Communication is key

- Try to be open and honest with each other, especially if there is tension.
- Take time to listen to each other.
- Make time for each other when you can. Try and spend some time together as a couple.
- Try to share the housework so you can have more time together.
- Try to have individual time with your baby – this will strengthen your bond with your baby as well as giving your partner some 'me-time'.

If you would like to talk to someone who is not a friend or a family member, speak to your GP. They can refer you for relationship counselling.

Dealing with visitors

Your family and friends often want to share in your joy after your baby is born. You may be eager to show off your beautiful baby!

Occasionally having visitors in your home can be stressful.

The following tips might keep visits stress-free:

Accept help

People are often eager to help after a new baby arrives. If you're comfortable with it, why not let them fold laundry or empty the dishwasher?

Take a moment for yourself

Many visitors will want to hold and cuddle your baby. Take the opportunity to have a shower or to drink a cup of tea while it is still hot.

Spread out your visitors

Spread out your guests over the coming days or weeks. It can be lovely but exhausting having visitors. Often large groups can be overwhelming.

Avoid spreading illness

Ask people who are sick not to visit.

Tricky visitors

If there is someone who you feel might outstay their welcome, consider alternatives. Meet them for a coffee in town, or perhaps visit them.

Don't worry about mess

Lower your standards! Most people will not be surprised to see a messy house when you have recently given birth, especially if they are parents themselves.

Clean clothes on standby

Have comfy clean clothes on standby. This will help you feel better about yourself even if you have not had time to shower.

Health checks for your baby in the first 6 weeks

Your baby will get at least three health checks in the first six weeks after birth. These are covered under the Maternity and Infant Care Scheme and are free of charge.

Public health nurse postnatal check

Who:	Your public health nurse (PHN)
When:	Your midwife will tell your PHN about your baby's birth. If your baby was born in a hospital, the visit usually takes place within 72 hours of your discharge.
Where:	The PHN will usually visit your home.
What happens during the check:	The PHN will assess both your health and your baby's. They are there to offer you support. They will give you information on caring for your baby and advice on parenting. They will tell you about local resources like mother and baby groups or breastfeeding support groups. You may get more home visits if you need them. The PHN is available at your local health centre. They will continue to see you and your baby at different times over the next three-and-a-half years.

2-week check

Who:	Your general practitioner (GP) or the practice nurse in the GP surgery
When:	When your baby is 2 weeks old. You will need to book the appointment. Tell the receptionist that it is for a 2-week check for your baby.
Where:	You will need to attend your GP surgery for this visit.
What happens during the check:	Your GP or practice nurse will talk about your birth experience. They may: • undress and weigh your baby • check the appearance of your baby's skin for signs of poor circulation • talk to you about any concerns you may have • make sure your baby has had screening tests • check the umbilical cord • talk about vaccines

6-week baby check

Who:	Your GP
When:	When your baby is 6 weeks old.
Where:	You will need to attend the GP surgery for this visit.
What happens during the check:	Your GP will weigh your baby. They will measure their head, and may measure their length.

Your GP will examine your baby from head to toe. In particular they will check your baby's:

- eyes
- heart
- hips
- testes if your baby is a boy

They may give you advice on feeding, weaning, keeping your baby safe and vaccines.

Don't forget that mothers should have a check-up with their GP at 6 weeks too! See page 210.

When to get help for your baby

Trust your instincts. If you are worried about your child, do not hesitate to contact your GP or public health nurse for advice.

Many GPs will give advice over the phone or will try to fit a baby or young child in without an appointment.

Never worry about bothering them. They would prefer to advise you now and prevent a child getting seriously unwell later.

When to get help immediately

Contact your GP or nearest hospital emergency department (A&E) immediately if your baby:

- is hard to wake, unusually drowsy or does not seem to know you
- turns blue or very pale
- is breathing unusually, either faster or slower than usual, or grunting
- has a purple or red rash that looks unusual or that does not fade and lose colour when pressed, or
- has a sunken or raised fontanelle (the soft spot on their head)

When to get help today

Contact your GP today if your baby:

- has a fever, or feels unusually cold or floppy
- has an unusual or high-pitched cry
- has any unexplained bleeding or bruising
- suddenly develops jaundice or has jaundice for more than 2 weeks after birth
- has a hoarse cough with noisy breathing or is wheezing
- is not taking feeds
- is vomiting most of their feeds or has a lot of diarrhoea, or
- is not gaining weight or is losing weight

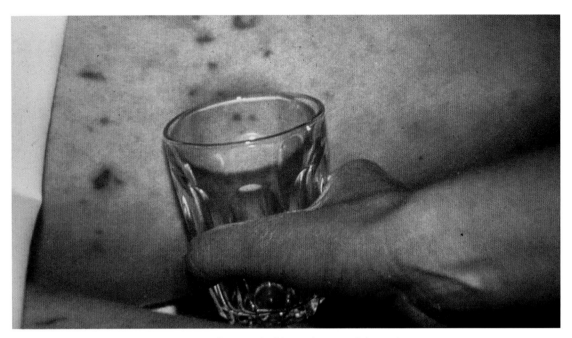

Photo: Meningitis Research Foundation. See meningitis.org for more information

The glass test for meningitis

Meningitis is a very serious illness. It is an infection of the lining of the brain and spinal cord. Symptoms can include a rash, but not always.

The glass test can help you decide if a baby's rash is suspicious.

Press the side or bottom of a glass firmly against the rash. This should cause the rash to fade and lose colour.

If it doesn't change colour, go to your GP immediately.

If you cannot get in touch with your GP or GP Out of Hours Service, bring your child to your nearest emergency department that treats children.

Save your GP's phone number and your local GP Out of Hours Service on your phone. Write them down somewhere accessible.

Make sure that anyone who looks after your baby has your GP's number.

Recovering from giving birth

Your period returning

Many women who breastfeed do not have a period until at least 6 months after giving birth. Some find that their periods do not return until after they have stopped breastfeeding. Mothers who do not exclusively breastfeed usually find that their period returns within two months.

Exercise

Being active will improve your health and your mood. It may help your recovery. Try to fit in a walk with your baby and any exercises the midwives or physiotherapists showed you.

Start slowly

Your body is still recovering from the pregnancy and birth. Start slowly and build up gradually. A slow 10 minute walk can be a good place to start. Slowly increase the time and the distance you walk. Low impact exercise like walking is recommended for the first 6 to 12 weeks after birth.

Leaking urine

Contact your GP or midwife if you notice that you are leaking urine (wee). They can refer you to see a physiotherapist with an interest in women's health.

Deep abdominal strengthening exercise

You can try this deep abdominal strengthening exercise when you feel strong enough:

1. Lie on your side with your knees slightly bent.
2. Let your tummy relax and breathe in gently.

3. As you breathe out, gently draw in the lower part of your stomach like a corset, narrowing your waistline.

4. Squeeze your pelvic floor.

5. Hold for a count of 10, then gently release. Repeat 10 times.

Healthy eating and weight

Now is a great opportunity to get to a healthy weight, no matter what your pre-pregnancy weight was. This will improve your energy.

No drastic measures

It is better to be a healthy weight before becoming pregnant again. However, now is not the time for drastic attempts to lose weight. Do not do crash diets.

Healthy food to hand

Life with a newborn can be very tiring. Try and have healthy foods to hand for when your energy slumps or get hungry.

- Eat healthy foods and reduce your intake of sugary or fatty foods.
- Drink lots of water.
- Breastfeeding will help burn calories, which helps lose the weight you gained. It also makes you feel hungry, so have healthy food choices available.
- Try not to have junk food in the house – if it is not there, you can't eat it.

Be patient. It took time for your body to grow a baby. It will take time to get back into shape!

Having sex

It is safe to have sex once the bleeding from your vagina has stopped and any wounds or stitches between your legs have healed.

You may not feel ready immediately. The exhaustion of having a newborn baby can affect your sex drive initially.

If it hurts

Contact your GP, GP practice nurse or public health nurse if it hurts to have sex. They can examine you and refer you to a specialist women's health physiotherapist.

Contraception

It is possible to become pregnant again even if your periods have not returned. If this is not what you would like, talk to your GP about contraception. See page 212.

Emotional changes after giving birth

Pregnancy and birth are profoundly emotional experiences. Having a newborn baby is exhilarating, exhausting and physically challenging. The sense of responsibility can be daunting. The sense of inadequacy and guilt can be overwhelming.

The baby blues

The baby blues are very common and are considered normal. They usually begin on day 3 after your baby has been born. You may be more tearful and emotional than normal. You may be irritable and feel isolated, vulnerable and lonely.

You may feel like you are on an emotional rollercoaster, going between great joy and great sadness. Although unpleasant, these feelings are short-lived. They usually pass in 1 to 2 weeks.

Postnatal depression

You could have postnatal depression if:

- feelings of 'baby blues' get worse or last for longer, or
- your mood becomes very low several months after your baby is born

You are not alone

It is thought that 10 to 15% of new mothers will develop postnatal depression.

It can last for months or even years if it is not treated. Your family and friends may notice that you have postnatal depression before you do.

Signs and symptoms of postnatal depression

You may be feeling sad, anxious and alone. You may be feeling guilty, irritable and angry. You may be experiencing panic attacks. You may not enjoy being with people, even your baby.

Other symptoms of postnatal depression include:

- crying easily
- feeling rejected by your baby
- worrying a lot about your baby
- loss of appetite
- feeling inadequate
- feeling tired all the time
- problems sleeping (insomnia)

Remember, you are not a bad mother.

Get help from your GP or public health nurse if:
- these feelings or symptoms last for more than 2 weeks, or
- you have any thoughts of harming yourself or your baby

You will feel like yourself again

The most important thing you can do is ask for help. Talk to your partner, family and friends. Talk to your GP or public health nurse. Try and explain to them exactly how you feel. Trust that you will feel like yourself again.

Eat well and try and get some exercise. Ask family and friends for help. Don't put too much pressure on yourself with housework and other chores, Focus on yourself and your baby.

Your GP may refer you for counselling or may prescribe medication. Remind your GP if you are breastfeeding. Some medication is not suitable for women who are breastfeeding.

Many public health nurses will screen for postnatal depression. They will tell you what support is available in your area.

Postpartum psychosis

Postpartum psychosis is a rare form of mental illness that affects 1 in 500 new mothers. It is also called postnatal or puerperal psychosis.

This term describes a form of mental illness where you lose touch with reality. Symptoms tend to begin shortly after birth, and can include restlessness, agitation and confusion. This type of postnatal mood change often needs hospital treatment.

A note for partners about postnatal depression

Living with someone with postnatal depression can be extremely worrying. There are things you can do to help:

- Know the signs and symptoms of postnatal depression.
- Encourage your partner to get help and offer to go with her to appointments.
- Make sure she eats enough and gets rest.
- Encourage her to do some exercise.
- Take the baby out for a walk to give her a break.
- Plan activities as a couple away from the baby.
- Listen to her.
- Ask family and friends for practical support, like making meals or doing laundry.
- Limit the number of visitors.
- Tell her she is a great mother and doing great.
- Find out if there are any support groups or mother and baby groups in your area.

Take care of yourself too. Life with a new baby is stressful, especially if the baby's mother is unwell with postnatal depression.

- Find someone to talk to.
- Take some time for yourself – you need a break too.

Research has shown that up to 10% of partners experience depression after the birth of a child. Speak to your GP if you are feeling down, depressed or anxious for more than 2 weeks.

Support groups

Postnatal Depression Ireland: 021 492 2083, pnd.ie

Samaritans 24hr listening service: 116 123 (you don't need to put an area code before the number), samaritans.org

Parentline: 1890 92 72 77, parentline.ie

Cuidiú-Irish Childbirth Trust: 01 872 4501, cuidiu-ict.ie

Aware: 1800 80 48 48, aware.ie

Grow: 1890 474 474, grow.ie

See yourmentalhealth.ie for more information on support.

When to get medical help after the birth

It is normal to feel sore or tender after giving birth. There are some things you should look out for after giving birth, as you may need medical help.

Contact your GP, public health nurse or midwife immediately if you have:

- heavy vaginal bleeding or large clots coming from your vagina and feel dizzy or weak – these can be signs of postpartum haemorrhage
- smelly vaginal discharge – this can be a sign of infection
- pain in your tummy, especially if it is severe – this can be a sign of infection
- a fever, especially if your temperature is over 38°C
- any problems with a wound or stitches like redness, pus or if the wound seems to be opening
- headache, blurred vision or vomiting – these can be signs of pre-eclampsia
- any symptoms of postnatal depression or any thoughts of harming yourself or your baby (see page 206)
- pain when you wee, passing urine more often or smelly urine – these can signs of a urinary tract infection
- any worries or you feel something is not right

It is also important to contact your GP, midwife or physiotherapist if you have:

- difficulty controlling urine (wee) or poo for more than 6 weeks after the birth, or
- any symptoms of prolapse such as feeling something coming down or bulging in your vagina.

Postnatal check-up

Make an appointment for your postnatal check-up for 6 weeks after the birth of your baby. This check-up is part of the Maternity and Infant Scheme and free of charge.

This may be done by your GP or obstetrician. It will be done at the same time as your baby's 6 week check if done by your GP.

The aim of this check is to make sure you are recovering from giving birth and feeling well.

It is a good chance for the GP to meet the newest member of your family. It is also a chance for you to voice any concerns you may have and to ask questions. Consider making a list of any questions you may have before the appointment.

What to expect from this check

Your doctor will talk you about:

- any concerns you have
- the birth
- how breastfeeding is going for you and your baby
- postnatal depression
- contraception

Physical checks

The doctor will check your blood pressure and, usually, your weight.

A vaginal or 'internal' examination is not routinely done. However, your doctor will examine you if you have any concerns about how well you are healing.

Don't be embarrassed to talk to your doctor if you are leaking urine or poo, or if sex hurts. These are common problems that can be treated.

Cervical screening

If you are due a cervical screening test (smear test), you can discuss this. Normally a smear test is not done until 3 months after giving birth.

Low rubella levels

If your antenatal bloods showed low rubella levels, you will be offered the MMR (measles, mumps and rubella) vaccine.

Thinking about another baby?

If you are hoping to get pregnant again soon, your chances are far better if you and your partner are in good health. It can take up to a year to conceive, even if you got pregnant quickly the last time.

> ### What to start doing if you want to get pregnant
>
> - Take folic acid every day – ideally start at least 3 months before you become pregnant and keep taking it until you are at least 12 weeks pregnant.
> - Be a healthy weight – this improves your chances of getting pregnant and having a healthy pregnancy. Avoid crash diets. Follow a healthy balanced diet and do exercise.
> - Stop risky habits like smoking and binge drinking.
> - Speak with your doctor about any prescription medication that you are taking. Certain medications can be dangerous to take during pregnancy.
> - Get the MMR (measles, mumps, and rubella vaccine). If you are not immune to rubella, get it at least one month before you try to get pregnant. Rubella (German measles) can damage your developing baby.
> - Talk to your GP or consultant if you have a chronic illness like diabetes, epilepsy or autoimmune disease.

Family planning and contraception

Some women are keen to become pregnant again soon after giving birth. Some prefer to leave several years between babies. For others, their family is complete and they do not desire another pregnancy.

Contraceptives can be short-acting or long-acting.

Short-acting

Short-acting contraceptives are best if you think you may want another baby soon.

These include:

- male condoms - these are the only form of contraception that will protect you from sexually transmitted infections (STIs)
- caps and diaphragms
- progesterone-only pill ('mini pill')
- combined oral contraceptive pill ('the pill')
- contraceptive patch
- contraceptive ring

Long-acting

Long-acting contraceptive methods are much more than effective than short-acting.

They are suitable if you wish to space out your pregnancies or if your family is complete.

Long-acting contraceptives include:

- contraceptive injection
- contraceptive implant ('the bar')
- intrauterine system (IUS) - this is sometimes called 'the coil'
- intrauterine contraceptive device (IUD) or 'copper coil'
- permanent or irreversible methods like vasectomy (male sterilisation) and tubal ligation (female sterilisation)

Long-acting methods are much more reliable than short-acting methods. Using long-acting methods is the best way to prevent an unplanned pregnancy.

Things to remember when choosing contraception

Some methods are more effective than others. Some may be unsuitable if you are overweight or have certain medical conditions.

Your GP will help you decide which method suits you. You may need to arrange a special appointment to have coils or implants fitted.

Which contraceptives can be used while breastfeeding?

✔ Male condoms.

✔ Caps and diaphragms.

✔ Progesterone-only pill ('the mini pill').

✔ Contraceptive injection.

✔ Contraceptive implant ('the bar').

✔ Intrauterine system (IUS) – 'the coil'.

✔ Intrauterine device (IUD) – 'copper coil'.

✗ Combined oral contraceptive pill ('the pill').

✗ Contraceptive patch.

✗ Contraceptive ring.

For more information on contraception and sexual health, see sexualwellbeing.ie

Coping with loss – stillbirth and neonatal death

When a baby is delivered after 24 weeks or more of pregnancy and is not alive, this is known as a stillbirth. Neonatal death is when a baby dies within the first 28 days of being born.

Every year in Ireland approximately 500 babies die around the time of birth. Often the causes of these deaths are not known. It is devastating to lose a baby in this way.

When the baby dies in the womb

Sometimes the baby dies in the womb but labour does not start immediately. If this happens, you will be given medications to induce the labour. This is the safest way for you to give birth to your baby and it means that you and your partner can see and hold the baby at birth if this is what you want.

Emotions

It is a shock for parents when their baby dies. You may be asked to make important decisions, which can be extremely difficult at such an emotional time. Emotions that you experience can include disbelief, anger, guilt and grief. Do not feel pressurised into doing anything you are not comfortable with.

Give yourself time. You need to grieve. Everyone grieves in their own way. This may be a longer or shorter period of time for different people.

Telling other children

If you have other children, it is important to talk to them about their brother or sister who has died. Every child reacts differently. Sometimes feelings of grief are expressed through tantrums and other difficult behaviours.

For more information and support

Feileacain, the Stillbirth and Neonatal Death Association of Ireland: feileacain.ie

A Little Lifetime Foundation: alittlelifetime.ie

Benefits and entitlements

It is a good idea to be aware of the various supports available to pregnant women and to parents.

Antenatal classes

You are entitled to take paid time off work to attend antenatal classes (page 23). Expectant fathers have the right to attend two antenatal classes.

Antenatal appointments

You can also take time off for antenatal appointments.

Maternity leave

All pregnant employees can take maternity leave for a basic period of 26 weeks.

You need to:

- start your maternity leave at least 2 weeks before your estimated due date
- take at least four weeks after the birth of your baby

You can also get 16 weeks' unpaid maternity leave as well as your paid entitlement.

Maternity benefit

You may be entitled to a payment known as maternity benefit. This depends on your social insurance contributions.

Parental leave

When you return to work, or are due to return, you can also choose to take parental leave. Both parents are entitled to take parental leave. See citizensinformation.ie for the latest information on parental leave.

Paternity leave

Partners or spouses living with you can take paid paternity leave of 2 weeks following a birth or adoption. Paternity leave can be started at any time within the first 6 months after the arrival of the baby.

Paternity benefit

Paternity benefit is a payment to employed and self-employed people who are on paternity leave from work.

It is paid for 2 weeks and covered by social insurance (PRSI). There are a number of conditions you need to satisfy to get it.

Child benefit

After your baby's birth is registered, you can get child benefit. This is paid on the first day of the month after the child is born.

Maternity cash grant

If you have a medical card, you are entitled to a maternity cash grant from the HSE after the birth of your child.

Speak to your Department of Social Protection's community welfare officer if your income is not enough to meet the needs of your baby. See welfare.ie

One parent family payment

Contact the Department of Social Protection if you are parenting alone. You may be entitled to the one-parent family benefit.

Under-6s GP card

All children under 6 years of age living in Ireland can get a GP visit card. See hse.ie

Breastfeeding mothers

If you are breastfeeding a baby under the age of 6 months, you are entitled to take time off at work each day to breastfeed.

For more information, see citizensinformation.ie and welfare.ie

Going back to work after maternity leave

Many parents want or need to return to work after giving birth. It is very important to make the decision that suits you and your family best.

Going back to work after maternity or paternity leave can be difficult. Here are a few tips to make it easier:

Childcare

Organise childcare well in advance. You will be less stressed if you are comfortable with your childcare arrangements. This might be at a crèche, child-minder or family member.

Settling in

Introduce your baby to the childcare provider several weeks before you go back to work. Begin the process of 'settling in'. Make sure your baby has had plenty of time to settle in before you go back to work.

Most childcare providers are well used to anxious parents. They will have routines for getting a baby used to their surroundings. Follow their advice, but ask for more time if you need it.

Breastfeeding

Try to get your baby used to taking milk from a bottle or a cup before you return to work. If you decide to express breast milk (see page 150) during work hours, think how you are going to pump and store the milk.

Share the housework

If you have a partner, they may have grown used to you being at home most of the time and doing many of the chores. Talk about this before you go back to work. Plan how to split household tasks fairly.

See if there are ways to outsource some chores.

Good quality time with your baby

Make sure you fit in ways to spend good quality time with your baby. This can be difficult when you are exhausted after work, and when your baby is tired too.

Instead of delaying bedtime and then rushing, start the bedtime routine at your usual time. Take your time bathing them and reading to them. Enjoy the cuddles.

Spend some time planning

Anything you can plan in advance makes the morning rush less stressful. For example, plan meals or outfits for you and your baby.

As one journey ends, another begins

As the journey through pregnancy and birth ends, your journey as a parent is just beginning.

This is a rewarding and exciting chapter. But it can be a tiring, stressful and even a frustrating journey at times!

We hope that this booklet has helped prepare you for your pregnancy, your baby's birth and for the early weeks of becoming a parent.

You know your baby best

Sometimes you might feel overwhelmed by:

- the amount of choices before you
- the decisions you have to make

Remember to trust your instincts. You know your baby better than anyone else. You know what to do, and do what is right for you. As long as your baby is safe, there are very few 'wrong' choices.

Don't be too hard on yourself. All parents need to 'learn on the job'. All you can do is be the best parent that you can be.

Ask questions and get support

Never be afraid to ask questions or share your concerns with healthcare professionals, no matter how silly they seem. Your doctors, midwives and nurses are there to help and support you.

Try to get as much support as you can from friends and family members.

Time for you

Try to carve out time for yourself and look after your own needs, as well of the needs of your new little alarm clock!

Finally

Parenthood changes you, in big ways and small ways. As most parents will tell you, it is all worthwhile.

> Your public health nurse will give you the next book in this series,
> My Child: 0 to 2 years.

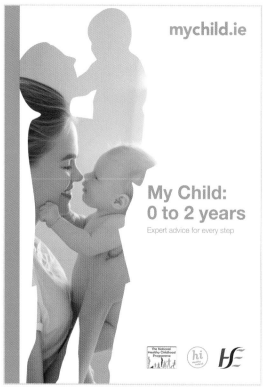

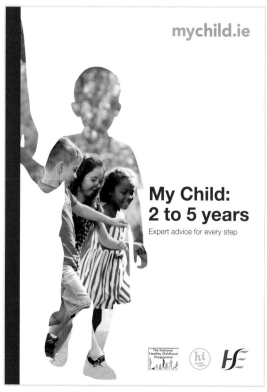

Index

Index

Index

Index

Standing on the shoulders of giants

The authors of this book wish to acknowledge the following publications and resources that provided us with inspiration as well as information:

Health and Social Care (2014). The Pregnancy Book. Public Health Agency. Belfast.

Best Start Resource Centre (2016). A Healthy Start for Baby and Me. Toronto, Ontario, Canada

HSE (2015). Information on Preparing for Birth & Parenthood. Cork University Maternity Hospital. CUMH. Cork

National Maternity Hospital Community Midwives (2015). Pregnancy Information. Dublin.

Hatkoff, A. (2007). You are my World. New York: Stewart, Tabori & Chang.

Nugent, K. (2011). Your Baby is Speaking to you. Boston, Mass.: Houghton Mifflin Harcourt.

Stern, D., Bruschweiler-Stern, N. and Freeland, A. (1998). The Birth of a Mother. New York: Basic Books.

NCP Obs & Gynae National Clinical Guidelines. Accessed at: https://www.hse.ie/eng/about/who/cspd/ncps/obstetrics-gynaecology/resources/national-clinical-guidelines/

Royal College of Obstetricians and Gynaecologists. Patient Information Leaflets. Accessed at: https://www.rcog.org.uk/en/patients/patient-leaflets/

Wyevalley.nhs.uk. (2018). [online] Available at: https://www.wyevalley.nhs.uk/media/187230/SALT-LEAFLET-talking-to-your-baby-BUMP-Job-No1238.pdf

RCOG Guidelines http://www.sgh-og.com/guidelines/rcog-green-top-guidelines/